A REMARKABLE MOTHER

JIMMY CARTER

THORNDIKE PRESS
A part of Gale, Cengage Learning

GALE
CENGAGE Learning·

Detroit • New York • San Francisco • New Haven, Conn • Waterville, Maine • London

Thorndike Press® Large Print Biography.

The text of this Large Print edition is unabridged.

Other aspects of the book may vary from the original edition.

Set in 16 pt. Plantin.

Printed on permanent paper.

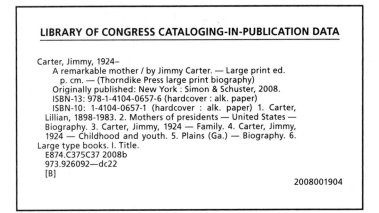

LIBRARY OF CONGRESS CATALOGING-IN-PUBLICATION DATA

Carter, Jimmy, 1924–
    A remarkable mother / by Jimmy Carter. — Large print ed.
      p. cm. — (Thorndike Press large print biography)
    Originally published: New York : Simon & Schuster, 2008.
    ISBN-13: 978-1-4104-0657-6 (hardcover : alk. paper)
    ISBN-10: 1-4104-0657-1 (hardcover : alk. paper) 1. Carter,
Lillian, 1898-1983. 2. Mothers of presidents — United States —
Biography. 3. Carter, Jimmy, 1924 — Family. 4. Carter, Jimmy,
1924 — Childhood and youth. 5. Plains (Ga.) — Biography. 6.
Large type books. I. Title.
    E874.C375C37 2008b
    973.926092—dc22
    [B]

                                    2008001904

Published in 2008 in arrangement with Simon & Schuster, Inc.

To the memory of my parents,
Lillian Gordy Carter
and James Earl Carter, Sr.

In India, what I did was help people who didn't have anything. I'm not quoting the Bible because I don't know it that well, but it says that when you do something for somebody in need you get back a hundredfold. I got it back a thousandfold.

— LILLIAN CARTER,
PEACE CORPS VOLUNTEER

CONTENTS

Lillian Gordy, age fifteen

1
EARLY FAMILY YEARS

Bessie Lillian Gordy was born in Chatta-hoochee County, Georgia, the fifteenth day of August, 1898, and was one of the most extraordinary people I've ever known. She was the fourth of nine children, two of them adopted "double first cousins," and was described in news reports as "third cousin of U.S. Senators Jesse Helms and Sam Nunn, fourth cousin of Elvis Presley, and mother of President Jimmy Carter." We children thought this diverse heritage partially explained her interest in politics and show-manship, but not some of her other idiosyncrasies.

My mother's great-grandfather Wilson Gordy was the first of his family to be born in Georgia, in 1801. He was descended from Peter Gordy, who was born in Somerset County, Maryland, in 1710. We've never attempted to trace the genealogy further, but some of the older kinfolks always said that the Gordys came from France. Wilson moved to West Georgia near the Chattahoochee River in the 1830s, soon after the Lower Creek Indians were forced westward and land was opened to white settlers. All of his possessions were in a large hogshead, with an axle through the center, which rolled down the narrow openings through virgin timber, drawn by his only horse. He soon became known as the best carpenter of what would be Chattahoochee County. Lillian's grandfather James Thomas Gordy was a wagon master during the Civil War and later county tax collector, and he married Harriet Emily Helms, whose parents came from North Carolina.

Lillian's father was James Jackson Gordy, named after an early hero of Revolutionary War days, and he was always known as Jim Jack. A federal government revenue officer in Southwest Georgia and later postmaster in Richland, he became one of the most astute political analysts in his changing communities. Mama's mother was Mary Ida Nicholson, daughter of Nathaniel Nunn Nicholson and granddaughter of Frances Nunn, whose family moved from the Carolinas to Georgia soon after the Revolutionary War.

My grandfather Jim Jack was thirteen years old when the "Northern oppressors" finally relinquished political and economic control of the state in 1876, and it was inevitable that there was still a legacy of North-South bitterness among the older relatives in the earliest political discussions I ever heard. Slavery was never mentioned — only the unwarranted violation of states' rights and the intrusion of the federal government in the private lives of citizens. I remember that my mother was the only one in her family who ever spoke up to defend Abraham Lincoln.

I recorded some of my mother's comments about her family:

"Well, first of all let me tell you about Mama. She seemed to be real quiet, but she never let Papa push her around. For instance, Papa was quite a dandy when he was young. He was engaged to another woman in Cusseta before he even met my mother, and the wedding was all planned. I never did know if it was a forced wedding or not, but when the time came he got on the train and disappeared, leaving his bride standing at the altar. He stayed away about three months, then came back and started courting Mama. When they were engaged, he was twenty-five and she was just seventeen, but Mama was really feisty. She told him she wasn't going to even dress for the ceremony until she knew he was standing by and ready. She sat in a chair in the preacher's house, with her wedding dress on the bed, until Papa arrived at the church next door and the preacher came over and certified that he was there. Only then did she get up, put on her wedding dress, and join him for the ceremony.

"The newlyweds moved to a little settlement called Brooklyn, just a crossroad with about a dozen families, where Papa had his first job as schoolmaster. Mama always told us about the first meal she cooked. Papa brought home some oysters, and she said the more she boiled them the tougher they got.

"Mama took care of the house and all of us children, with not much help from Papa. She had three children one right after another, and then Papa's brother either was shot or killed himself, and Mama took his two boys, my double first cousins. They were Catholics, and we made fun of them when they knelt down to pray or said their catechism. So Mama had five babies at once, none old enough to go to bed without help. Then she skipped three years and I came along, followed by three more — all of us two or three years apart."

My grandmother Ida was calm, a homebody, and seemed to be perfectly satisfied with her way of life. She would spend all day in the house and garden, first preparing food for a big family, getting the children off to school, and cleaning the house. Then she would put on her sunbonnet and work in the large garden, bringing a basket full of seasonal vegetables back into the house.

She always cooked a big dinner at noon, including pies, cakes, or fruit puffs for a constant supply of dessert. After the dishes were washed, she would clean the kitchen, wash and iron the family's clothes, and take care of the kids coming home from school, being sure that they did their chores and completed their homework assignments. Then she had to prepare supper, including leftovers plus a few fresh-cooked items. She was up each morning at 4:30 and would light up the woodstove while Grandpa, if he was home and it was winter, would make a fire in the fireplace.

On Sundays, everyone went to Sunday School and church, so Grandma had to prepare most of the large dinner in advance, maybe cooking the biscuits and fried chicken after the services were over. For one afternoon a week, she joined some of the other ladies of the community in a quilting bee, all of them sewing while they discussed affairs of their families and the community. I can see now that hers was a complete life, not much different from that of most

Ida Nicholson Gordy, c. 1910

Southern women of the time. She was proud and grateful to serve the other members of her family, who more or less took her for granted, just helping with the chores when she asked them.

My mother told me, "At times when we were raised there were real hard times, but we got by. I can remember when Mama could send me to the store to get twenty-five cents' worth of steak and it would feed all nine of us."

My grandfather was as wide-roving and flamboyant as my grandmother was home-loving and quiet. He was born in 1863 near Columbus, Georgia, and taught school for several years in Brooklyn before moving ten more miles to the larger town of Richland. Jim Jack was a man's man. He was tall, slender,

Jim Jack Gordy, c. 1910

handsome, and always well groomed and neatly dressed. Even on workdays, he preferred to wear a bow tie — never a pre-tied one.

Jim Jack was totally committed to mastering the prevailing political situation, as his daughter, my mother, described proudly: "My father could tell you pretty close to what vote any man would get, not only in the county but even in the whole state. All my life when I was a girl, until I left home to be a nurse, I saw him do this. For local elections, he would write out his predictions of the outcomes and seal them in an envelope. The county clerk would put them in his safe, and then compare the results after votes were counted. But it was just interesting to me to see the lengths he would go to keep up with politics. They would come in droves to see him."

Grandpa — of necessity — also demonstrated a remarkable understanding of national elections. During years that long preceded a civil service system in the U.S. government, he was nimble enough on his political feet to guess right in several presidential elections, shifting party allegiance to retain his appointment as postmaster in Richland. Earlier, when Warren Harding was elected in 1920, Grandpa went to make arrangements for the position in the small town of Rhine, the only rural Republican stronghold, where federal appointments were dispensed because of political support — or bribes. They had already allotted the postmaster's position but promised Jim Jack the next appointment and gave him an interim job as chief revenue agent for our region. As a former schoolmaster, he kept meticulous records, and I still have one of his notebooks covering two months in 1922, showing that he destroyed thirty-six stills during that time.

Later, I heard my father say that this was one job for which Grandpa and his sons were especially qualified, having done business with most of the moonshiners in the area. Grandpa would take a "sociable" drink on frequent occasions, but I never knew him to be tipsy enough to lose his composure or bring ridicule on himself. He had two sons, though, who had serious problems with whiskey.

Jim Jack's only unswerving political allegiance was to Tom Watson, who was a Democratic congressman in North Georgia but was disavowed by his party when he advocated equal economic treatment for black and white workers and small farmers. Watson joined the Populist Party and in 1896 was nominated as vice president on William Jennings Bryan's Populist ticket. He was elected by Georgians to the U.S. Senate after he changed his political philosophy almost completely and ran on a racist platform.

My grandfather considered his own greatest achievement to be suggesting the concept of rural delivery of mail to Tom Watson, who got the proposal passed into law. Among mementos we inherited from Grandpa were letters between him and Watson on this subject, as well as Watson's biography of Thomas Jefferson, which, for some reason, was dedicated to the newspaper magnate William Randolph Hearst.

A couple of times each year, my mother would get word that "Papa has gone again." Grandpa would pack a small suitcase, get a supply of flour, meal, sugar, coffee, side meat, some liquid refreshments — and a good supply of books — and tell his wife, "Ida, I'm going out to the farm for a while." She had learned that protests were fruitless, so she would tell him good-bye and expect to see him again in two or three weeks. They owned a small, remote farm in Webster County near Kinchafoonee Creek with a tenant shack on it, mostly woodland with not enough open land to farm. It was a haven for Grandpa, away from the hurly-burly of home life. When he would finally tire of the solitude or feel that his official duties couldn't spare him longer, he would return home as though he had just been down at the drugstore, with no thought of apologies or explanations for his absence.

It was an accepted fact within our family that the Gordys couldn't get along with each other long enough to enjoy a full meal together. Sometimes on the way to Sunday dinner in Richland after church in Plains, Daddy and Mama would try to guess what would precipitate the main argument of the day. Although my father teased Mother about the Gordys' arguments, I don't remember his family ever having a Sunday meal together.

Grandpa Gordy was a restless man, always preferring to be somewhere else than with his own family or with boring companions. The only exception was my mother, whom he invited to serve as his assistant in the post office until she moved from Richland to Plains. Jim Jack finally lost his government job in 1932, when Franklin D. Roosevelt was elected, and had to become a dirt farmer, trying to support his family on a hardscrabble farm that he rented not too far from where we lived near Plains. I remember him, tall and slender, wearing overalls with a buttoned shirt and a bow tie, walking behind a mule-drawn plow in a futile attempt to control Bermuda grass in a scraggly cotton field.

Recently I found a small homemade diary book that Grandma Gordy kept from March 1932 until August 1936, during the depths of the Great Depression. The occasional entries concentrate on the status of her children, especially Tom, who was traveling all over the Pacific Ocean in the navy. During the time they were farming near Plains, one entry was extraordinarily personal: "Papa is somewhat peeved tonight about his mule, afraid he is sick. He said if the mule died I would have to look out for myself. I said I hope he dies then. He knew I did not mean that, but seems like I just can't say a word lately but what he takes it for the worst. Such is life." Then she wrote, "I should not have written the above, but have no rubber on my pencil to spoil it out."

Later, she wrote, "The old mule died Friday. This is two mules to die since we've been here. We will get along some way. God will not forsake us." Another entry, in February 1935, describes a notable characteristic of her husband: "J.J. has gone to Richland. Seems it would make him sick to not be going all the time. He loves to be on the go."

My mother always remained very proud of her special relationship with Grandpa. She told me, "There was no doubt that I was Papa's favorite. Everyone in the family knew it. I guess one reason was that I didn't always accept what he said as the gospel truth, and would argue with some of his opinions. Looking back, I see that I was always careful not to go too far with it, and to back off if it looked like he was getting too aggravated. In a lot of cases, though, particularly when he and I were alone at the post office, I think he liked for me to speak up so we could have something of a debate.

"I read more than anyone else in the family — except him, of course — and I tried to learn about things that interested him. Sometimes he would give me a book he had just read, and we both looked forward to a fierce discussion about the subject. One thing I liked about working at the post office was that both of us could find time to read on the job. Another thing was that we probably knew more than anybody else about what was going on around Richland. Papa handled a lot of telegraph messages, and taught telegraphy to two of his sons. He had a way of absorbing the news, but always cautioned me about not repeating gossip we heard if it would hurt anyone. I loved Mama and Papa, but I have to admit that I was ready to leave home and go in nurses' training, and when I got to Plains I didn't go back very often."

I remember that after I graduated from the U.S. Naval Academy, in 1946, I borrowed my daddy's automobile and drove the eighteen miles from Plains to Richland. I stopped by my grandparents' home and enjoyed some sweet milk and blackberry pie while telling Grandma about my new career. She then told me that Jim Jack was downtown in Richland, "probably at the drugstore." I walked there and, sure enough, found my grandfather with some other loafers assembled around one of the glass-topped tables, drinking Cokes and engaged in a heated discussion of some local issue. I stood behind him for a few minutes, until one of the men noticed my uniform and indicated my presence to Grandpa.

When he turned around, I could tell that he didn't recognize me, and I blurted out, "Grandpa, I'm Jimmy, Lillian's son." He shook my hand and said, "Boy, I'm real glad to see you again." Then he turned back and continued his conversation. I stood there a few minutes, then went back home and off to my first ship. That was the last time I saw him before he died a few months later.

The temperaments of the younger Gordys mirrored the stark differences in the characters of their parents. The girls had professional careers, married well, and raised fairly stable families, in some ways like their mother, but the boys were more like Grandpa — without his reading habits, interest in politics, or self-restraint regarding alcohol.

2
NURSING AND MARRIAGE
IN PLAINS

Mama received a much better education than most other girls her age because of her constant reading and her determination to pursue a medical career. She said, "I signed up to be a nurse when the army was asking for nurses. That was in 1917, when I was nineteen, and I was very patriotic. The day the armistice was signed was when I received my letter of acceptance, but immediately the army did away with the program."

Everyone in the region knew about the fine Wise Sanitarium in Plains, which included an active training program for medical interns and registered nurses. Mama applied, despite opposition in her family to her leaving home, and was accepted. "In those days nurses were not like they are now," she said. "Nurses made little money and were not highly respected. They were thought of as servants, often improperly abused or even seduced by doctors."

My mother moved to Plains in 1920, eager to trade her job in the Richland post office for a career in medicine. At least for one reason, this was an opportunity that she and most of her family welcomed. At twenty-two years of age, she had already heard her mother and older sisters say, "Lilly, you don't want to be an old maid." She later told us children that she had not been averse to combining marriage with her new career. She wasn't completely innocent when she left Richland. She later told a news reporter, "My mother was not very modern — not liberated like me. She was a wonderful woman, but very old-fashioned. Until I was twenty-one, I never even got into a car or a buggy by myself if there was a boy in it. I always had a chaperone." She winked. "I learned everything I know from that chaperone."

Her first date in Plains was with George Tanner, a big, rough-looking sawmill man who had a sister named Lucy. They decided to go dancing at Magnolia Springs, a resort near Plains, and Lucy went with a local grocer named Earl Carter. Lillian had seen Earl once before, swimming in the pool and ostentatiously doing front flips and half gainers off the springboard into the frigid water. She had considered him a smart aleck and a show-off, and wasn't pleased to have him

Earl Carter, army officer trainee, 1915

along. Her dislike was intensified when he asked her to dance just once during the entire evening, and then only when urged on by George Tanner and just to be courteous.

One of our favorite shared pastimes as children was to have Mama tell us about the days before we were born. In the warm months, my sisters and I would sit on the front porch or the steps, and in wintertime we would be near the living room fire. The routine, which both Mama and we enjoyed, would begin with our chanting, "Tell us a story!" After some friendly delay (and with Daddy aloof from the process, maybe reading his newspaper nearby), we would call out different subjects — "How you and Daddy met," "About Grandpa and Grandma," "When we were born," or "The time you did so-and-so" — until a consensus evolved. To us, these accounts were better than fairy tales, and we would press Mama with questions to expand her earlier tellings of the same happenings. When my sisters were young, Mama usually addressed her remarks to me, and I was the one who probed for more and more information. To some degree, our kinfolks became mythical characters through these tale-telling hours, so that when we met them later, we knew a lot more than they could have dreamed, at least about our mother's impressions of them.

In a later taped conversation, Mama described Earl Carter's situation at the time she met him: "After being with him at that Magnolia Springs dance, I couldn't stand him. (Don't put that in your notes!) He was working for his brother, Alton, and running a pressing club down on the main street. With a Negro man helping him, Earl claimed he was making a hundred dollars a month."

The following week, Lillian and some other student nurses were walking from their storefront dormitory toward the drugstore when they passed a group of young men. Earl was among them, and he soon came into the pharmacy and approached the trainees at the soda fountain. He tipped his hat and said, "Good morning, Miss Gordy, it's good to see you again." She nodded, and he asked, "May I speak with you for a moment?"

When they stepped aside, he asked if she would like to go for a ride that weekend. She agreed, and they set a time for him to pick her up. She quickly learned that some of the other nurses knew several things about her prospective date. "They said he was pretty fast with women, liked to play baseball and poker, and owned an open-topped Model T Ford."

We always liked to hear Mama describe that outing: "For some reason, I was nervous and excited, and began to worry about what I would wear. I finally borrowed a navy blue taffeta dress from Miss Pennington, one of the other nurses. All of us wore uniforms most of the time and swapped our regular clothes with each other when we had a date. I peeked over our balcony above the main street when Earl parked his car, and I made him come upstairs to call for me.

"It was a little before sundown, and he said he was going to drive out toward Preston and show me the farmland his family owned. I reckon he wanted to make an impression regarding how well-off they were. We hadn't got to Choctahatchee Creek before it started pouring down rain, and the car didn't have a top. He had a real thick wool lap robe, though, and we covered up as best we could and he drove on over to the farm and parked under a wagon shed until it quit raining."

With just a slight smile, she continued: "We were pretty well acquainted by the time we got back to town, and after that we began to date regularly. I could play the piano some, and Earl pretended to like to hear me, especially the 'Twelfth Street Rag.'"

Earl told Lillian that he had attended Riverside Academy through the tenth grade and then sold "flattening irons" in Oklahoma for a few months before giving that up and moving back to Plains. Then he went off to the army, became a first lieutenant, and was later engaged to a woman named Maggie Jenkins, before they broke it off. Maggie's photograph in an old family album showed a striking brunette, who later became a college professor. Mama always described their separation simply by saying, "He got his ring back."

She also said, "I didn't let on that I knew

anything about him, and he told me that he was not only making a hundred dollars a month but would soon be selling ice from a little insulated icehouse he was building across the railroad. I was impressed with his 'get up and go.'"

After that, the couple drove often to the Carter farm in Webster County, being especially attracted for some reason to the most remote field, nearest the creek. Sixty years later, when Mama and I went over there to look at some growing peanuts or planted pine trees, Mama would tell me, "This is where Earl and I did most of our courting."

The nurses' quarters soon moved down the street to some small rooms above the drugstore, where Mrs. Gussie Abrams was their general supervisor and a tough disciplinarian.

"Earl was one of Miz Abrams's favorites," Mama recalled, "and she would let him come into the doctors' area every now and then to see me even when I was on duty. One day, he came to tell me that his baby sister, Jeannette, had just learned that she had to get married to Wade Lowery, and it almost broke his heart. While we were still sitting there, he asked me to marry him.

"I was ready right then, mainly to get out of training, which was a terrible life, but Earl insisted that I finish and become a registered nurse, which wouldn't be until the following June. I spent six months at Grady Hospital in Atlanta, and didn't have time to go back to Plains. I almost went crazy, and really hated it when Earl sent my engagement ring to Atlanta by one of the doctors. On graduation, Earl explained to Grady officials that we were to be married, and they let me take the state board examination without the usual waiting period."

My parents first rented a little room upstairs in the Wellons family home, with a balcony and some outside stairs going down to the ground. Mama said, "It was on the northeast corner of the house, and was the coldest place in the world. Alton gave us a kitchen cabinet, Oliver McDonald's store a cookstove, and Dr. Sam Wise a rocking chair. Earl already had his own bedroom furniture, the same one we later had in the country in the front room. We had to go outdoors to the privy, so we lived with a slop jar.

"That room is where we first learned that you would be born.*

* That house is now the Plains Bed & Breakfast Inn and the room has a brass marker on the door: THE CONCEPTION ROOM.

"We stayed there for several more months, until Dr. Sam Wise said I couldn't go up and down the stairs anymore. He was concerned about me, but also wanted me to continue working with him in the operating room. That's when we moved down the street to the Cooks' home, on the ground floor."

When the time came, my mother presumed that I would be born at home, as were all the other babies at that time, but Doctor Sam said there was an empty room in the hospital, and she might come back to work quicker if he could deliver the baby there.* Mama never failed to mention that Daddy was out at a fish fry and poker game when she began having labor pains and didn't get home until real late to take her to the hospital.

"Someone gave us a little dog after you were born," she remembered, "and we had a big argument about it with Mrs. Cook, who made us leave her house. We moved two more times, and then Earl bought the house next door to Rosalynn Smith's family. That's the house we later swapped with the Plexicos, who built the home we owned out

---

* This made me the answer to a Trivial Pursuit question: "Who was the first U.S. president born in a hospital?"

in Archery, using plans obtained from Sears and Roebuck."

Whether Daddy was listening or not, Mama always gave us an unvarnished image of their early married life. "Earl was a twenty-nine-year-old bachelor, and he had his own way of doing things. He told me before we were married that he played poker every Friday night, but I figured I could break him of that. The first Friday after we were married he left right after supper and came home long after midnight. I refused to speak to him and pouted for a day or so, but it didn't do any good — then or later.

"I always accused him of being kinder to everyone else than he was to me. One time Ethel Wellons and I were both pregnant, and someone sent me some nice grapes. Earl said, 'Ethel is not feeling well, and I'd like to take the grapes to her,' so I threw them at him. When Gloria was real young, she got a beautiful doll, with movable eyes. Earl gave it to Margaret Timmerman, who was about six months older.

"That first Christmas, he went over to Plains Mercantile Co. at the last minute and bought me a lap robe. I was really mad that he didn't get me something more nice and personal. Before we were married he had given me a card case and a purse with three coins inside: a twenty-, a ten-, and a five-dollar gold piece. It was the most money I had ever had at one time. Someone in the nurses' home stole it — we were pretty sure who it was but never got it back."

Mama continued: "Then, in 1928, Earl bought the Plexico farm out at Archery, about two and a half miles west of Plains, and we moved out there when you were four years old. I remember we had to put you in through the front porch window to open the front door because we had forgotten the key. The most important thing that happened in that last house in Plains was that you pulled out the front drawers of a big chest of drawers and climbed up on them. The whole thing turned over on top of you. The mirror shattered all around you, but you weren't hurt at all." (Then Mama added, "Recently, Walter Cronkite and I were agreeing that you've always been lucky.")

"Earl kept the store in Plains for about three years after we moved to Archery, and he also had a café next door that other folks ran for him. Gloria was born while we were still in town, and Ruth was born after we moved to the country. Both of the girls were born at home — you and Billy in the hospital. Dr. Sam Wise delivered all four of you."

3
GROWING A FAMILY

The walls in our farmhouse were thin, and we children could hear some of our parents' arguments — on a relatively restrained level. When I was grown, after Daddy died, I asked Mama if they got along all right together. She said, "Sure we did — most of the time. But I must say that we had different ways, and it took us a long time to figure out how much room to give each other. Even after Gloria and Ruth came and I had started to slack off on nursing and was at home more, we still had our differences. As long as he lived, he still wanted to play poker once a week and also for him and me to go out on Saturday night and raise hell, and I got tired of it. As you know, he kind of took over the Elks Club in Americus, and claimed that he had to be there to make sure everything was run right. We would always have a few drinks, and he would dance with most of the pretty women in our crowd. I never was all that keen on dancing, and sometimes we had words afterward if he seemed to enjoy himself too much." It was obvious that, when faced with the ultimate choice of staying home alone, Mama usually chose to go out with Daddy.

Gloria and I learned quite early how best to deal with Daddy and Mama. He was a stern but fair disciplinarian, whose word was absolute law in our house. His two basic requirements were obedience and truthfulness, and any serious violations were punished with a switch on our legs. I can remember only five times when I received this punishment, but each of them — even after over seventy years — is still a vivid memory. When we realized that we would be caught doing something wrong, our best tactic was to confess to our mother, who supported the basic family discipline standards but was much more willing to forgive. If our misdeed was serious enough for Daddy to be informed, we were always eager to receive our punishment before he came home from work. After we had suffered a relatively mild spanking, we knew that Mama would say, "Now, Earl, I've already punished them."

Mama helped to provide a special background for our relatively protected and disciplined lives in Archery. I was born in

Lillian holding baby Jimmy, 1925

1924, Gloria two years later, and Ruth in 1929. Our brother, Billy, was a latecomer, thirteen years younger than I and only four years old when I left home to go to college and the navy. We siblings led separate lives. Except for family outings involving our parents, my two sisters and I had little in common during my earlier years. I was outside the house and even away from the yard whenever possible, with my father or my own playmates, and was increasingly employed with livestock and growing crops. Neither Mama nor my sisters ever worked in the barn lot, fields, or pastures, so while I was becoming familiar with axes, anvils, plowstocks, mules, cattle, and guns, they were involved with sewing machines, cooking utensils, dolls, dresses, and other mysterious feminine pursuits. We had meals together, and during early evening hours and rainy days we congregated in the living room.

Gloria was an independent spirit, the only one in our family who would overtly defy my father. Throughout our school years, she was larger than I, so we were competitive and often fought with each other. After college, Gloria became an accomplished bookkeeper and accountant, working for large landowners around the Plains area, and she and her husband, Walter Guy Spann, were avid motorcyclists, owning seven Harley-Davidsons at the time of her death.

Gloria had one son, William, who was a troubled child, and she spent most of her earnings on psychiatric care and special schools for him. On one occasion an instructor brought William and four other problem students to Plains, en route to a few days in Florida, and they spent the night at our cabin, the Pond House. A couple of hours after they left, the Pond House was destroyed by fire — either deliberately set or the result of a smoldering cigarette in a mattress. We never pursued an investigation, but Mother was especially distressed because my father (and I) had participated personally in its construction.

Gloria was something of a godmother to dozens of bikers, who would stop for a day or two at her home on the way to and from Daytona and other destinations farther south. When she died, of pancreatic cancer, her funeral procession was led by thirty-seven bikers, and her tombstone is inscribed, SHE RIDES IN HARLEY HEAVEN.

My younger sister, Ruth, always enjoyed a special status in our family. Although I was only five years old, I remember vividly when she had pneumonia and was expected to die. Mama was disturbed when Daddy lifted Ruth's inert little body from the crib. She cried out, "Earl, what in the world are you doing?"

He replied, "I'm going to let her see the sunshine one more time," and held her up to the window so she could look out into the yard. When he put her back on the pillow, we all knelt down and prayed for her. Ruth survived and thrived. From then on, although Ruth had her normal ups and downs with boyfriends and school affairs, she seemed to be sacrosanct. Ruth was a strong but gentle soul. Neither Daddy nor I ever had a significant disagreement with her, and she and I had a close and loving relationship throughout our lives.

After earning degrees in English and theology in North Carolina, Ruth became a famous author and evangelist. She ministered to the needs of a stream of troubled people both privately and at her counseling facility near Dallas, Texas. She also traveled throughout the world promoting her books and lecturing to large audiences about how to develop a joyful existence based on an intimate relationship with Jesus Christ. Both Gloria and my mother participated regularly in Ruth's ministry. Ruth was the closest friend of Rosalynn and was instrumental in orchestrating the early stages of our love affair. She, too, had pancreatic cancer and died at an early age.

Since I was away from Plains for twelve years at the U.S. Naval Academy and then in the navy, Billy grew up happily in Daddy's shadow and, had our father lived a few more years, would have assumed responsibility for the farmland and other family matters.

These plans were interrupted when I came home unexpectedly after my father's death, while Billy was still in high school. There were several years when Mama's primary task was to assuage Billy's resentment and to preserve harmony within the family. Despite her best efforts to keep him in Plains, Billy married and joined the U.S. Marines as a teenager, and it was not until several years later that he agreed to come back to Plains and become a partner with me and Mama in our growing agricultural supply business. Billy was extremely intelligent and a hard worker, and he had excellent rapport with our farmer customers. He assumed increasing management responsibilities as I pursued my relatively brief political career.

When I was campaigning for president, Billy represented our family at home in Plains, and with his independent spirit, wit, and sometimes excessive consumption of alcohol, he became a focus of news media attention. Once, when accused of being eccentric, he replied, "I've got one sister who spends all her time on a motorcycle, another who is a Holy-Roly preacher, a mother who was in the Peace Corps when she was seventy years old, and my brother thinks he's going to be President of the United States. Which one of our family do *you* think is normal?"

Mama often said that Billy was the smartest of her children, and none of us argued with her. He read at every possible moment — books, magazines, newspapers. Every morning when I arrived at the warehouse, at about 6:00 A.M., he had already absorbed all four newspapers that came to Plains. Billy was a walking encyclopedia on subjects that he found interesting, including international affairs, American politics, and especially baseball. He earned a lot of money betting with unsuspecting people who questioned his seemingly foolish comments, which always turned out to be factual.

Billy was a sober business executive during the last ten years of his life, and he and his wife, Sybil, used their nationwide popularity to counsel thousands of alcoholics on how to reform their lives. At the age of fifty-one, Billy succumbed to the same disease that killed his father and both his sisters.

We children, and our mother, were especially affected by two of her siblings. It was my mother's brother Tom Watson Gordy who helped shape my childhood ambition and my future life. Daddy was as well educated as necessary for the times, having completed the tenth grade at Riverside Academy and served as a military officer, but he was determined that I would realize what seemed, in those Depression years, to be a distant dream: to graduate from college. No one of our Carter ancestors had ever finished high school, and it seemed then that any college opportunities were limited to the two free military institutions, West Point and Annapolis. Although Daddy had served in the U.S. Army, he hadn't appreciated the experience enough to insist that I follow in his footsteps.

Uncle Tom had joined the navy when he was quite young, and he made a lifetime career of it. He was my distant hero, and through all the years of my boyhood, he and I wrote letters back and forth, mine giving news about the family and his, coming from the far reaches of the Pacific Ocean, filled with information about the exotic places his ships were visiting. I heard from him more than did anyone else in the family, and a letter or photograph from Uncle Tom was a memorable event in my young life that I was eager to share with my mother and the other Gordys. We all followed his career closely and were excited when he changed ships or made the slow advancement from boot camp to seaman and finally to radioman second class. The U.S. Navy had two rigid dirigibles, the *Macon* and the *Akron*, and Uncle Tom was part of the rescue team when the *Macon* went down in the waters near San Francisco. He sent Grandma a small piece of the aluminum hull, which she cherished for the rest of her life.

Uncle Tom was the champion lightweight boxer in the Pacific Fleet, and a photograph of him holding a trophy and standing in front of the men he had defeated occupied the central location on my grandparents' mantelpiece. He had a flat nose and curly hair, and walked with something of a strut, like James Cagney. He married a San Francisco girl named Dorothy, and they had three children during the 1930s, the oldest son named for me. It was Uncle Tom's service in the navy that captured my imagination, and my parents didn't object when this was my choice for a future career.

When the Japanese bombed Pearl Harbor, my uncle Tom and about thirty other sailors were stationed on Guam, part of the radio communications system that served the Pacific Fleet. With our military force incapacitated, it was inevitable that the island would be taken, and the men there were ordered not to resist. They were not trained for combat, at least in jungles, and it was likely that many Guamanians would suffer if the Japanese had to fight their way through the island. Tom and the others were captured when the war was only three days old and taken to Japan as prisoners. Tom's wife and their three children came to Georgia to stay with my grandparents, who were then living near us in Archery. Dorothy was a beautiful and quiet woman, but this life on a South Georgia farm was totally different from what she and the children had always known in San Francisco, and her city ways were considered strange by Tom's kinfolks.

In the summer of 1943, the International Red Cross notified Dorothy officially that Tom was dead, and she began receiving a widow's pension. Everyone was heartbroken, and she and the kids moved back to San Francisco to live with her parents. After a year or so, she married a friend of the family who had a stable job and promised to care for her and the children.

When the war ended two years later and American troops entered Japan, they found Tom Gordy still alive! He had been working for four years as a fireman on a small, isolated railroad that hauled coal from some mountain mines down to the main transportation lines. While they were Japanese prisoners, he and his fellow sailors had collected pieces of their clothing — red, white, and blue — to make a little American flag. Tom

47

brought it home with him.

He had been beaten and partially starved during those four years, weighed less than a hundred pounds, and was suffering from severe phlebitis. He was transferred back to a military hospital in Georgia for treatment, immediately promoted to lieutenant senior grade, and given all the back pay he would have earned.

I was in the navy at the time, and Tom wrote me about his situation and said that he still loved his wife and children and wanted to be with them. Dorothy quickly decided to have her second marriage annulled. I became furious when I learned that Tom, who was very weak, had been unable to resist Grandma, my mother, and his other sisters, who convinced him that Dorothy had betrayed him and committed adultery while he was a prisoner of war. They were divorced, and he was transferred to Florida and put in charge of security at a large navy base near Jacksonville.

Tom soon married a good second wife, was promoted to full commander, and when he retired he bought and operated a prosperous tavern. He visited us in Plains every now and then, and was proud when I was elected governor. He always reminded me that he had been two grades my senior in navy rank, but he died in 1975, not living to see me become commander in chief.

The other sibling of my mother's who was a great influence on me and the bright light in the Gordy family was my aunt Emily, whom everyone called Sissy. Only twelve years older than I, she was a frequent and welcome guest in our home, and my parents and I followed closely her education and early career as a teacher. The biggest social event that ever occurred at our house was Sissy's wedding party. We set up tables under shade trees in the front yard and borrowed folding chairs from the local funeral parlor. Mama decided that the main dish would be chicken salad, which could be prepared in advance from the large flock of hens and fryers in our yard. The guests could have a choice of sandwiches or a fuller meal served on dinner plates. My mother brought in several other women to help her prepare food for more than a hundred people, many of whom came all the way from Atlanta, the home of the groom.

The party got off to a fine start. Everyone was having a good time, and I was helping to replenish the supply of food on the tables. On one of my trips into the kitchen, I noticed a chicken flat on the ground near

49

the back steps, spasmodically kicking its legs. It died as I watched. I went to find my parents, and we began seeing other chickens perishing as well. We realized that the guests eating chicken salad would be even more distressed than we were when they saw the kinfolk of their food dying around their feet. Mama and Daddy had a secret consultation and told me and my friends to spread corn in the backyard to attract all the chickens and to pick up any dead and dying ones and hide them in the smokehouse. In the meantime, Mama would distract our guests and expedite their departure.

Mama was extremely concerned about what would happen to the guests a few hours later. Because of the scarcity of refrigeration, all the rural families were quite familiar with the threat of food poisoning, and we began preparing for the worst. We finished picking up all the feathered cadavers and had some hope restored when we found an open bag of nitrate of soda, which was used to fertilize the nearby cotton field, with a few chickens scratching and pecking around it. Daddy called my uncle Jack Slappey, the community's veterinarian, and he came out and confirmed our diagnosis of sodium nitrate poisoning. Our chicken salad did not threaten the lives of the wedding guests after all.

Sissy campaigned for me almost full-time during the 1976 presidential election, finally concentrating on Maine and helping me carry the state. Later, she organized and supervised about two hundred volunteers who worked at The Carter Center. At the same time, Sissy was honored as the most valuable citizen in her hometown of Roswell, Georgia. Her home, near Atlanta, was a haven for me when I was a student at Georgia Tech and a candidate for governor.

These were just two of my mother's kinfolks, and I presume that I inherited some of the characteristics of them all.

4
LIVING IN THE COUNTRY

Very few farm homes had a telephone when I was growing up, but there was one in our house. It was number 23, and we answered two rings. On the same party line, the Bacons had one ring and the Watsons picked up on three. (We presumed there were usually two listeners to all our calls.) We also seemed to have an omniscient operator in Plains, Miss Gladys Murray. If we placed a call to Mr. Roy Brannen, Miss Gladys would say, "He left for Americus this morning at about nine thirty, but he plans to be back before dinner. He'll probably stop by the stable, and I'll try to catch him there." She also had the latest news on any sickness in the community, plus a lot more information that indicated there were three listeners on most calls.

One significant difference between my parents was their reading habits. Daddy mostly limited his reading to the daily and weekly newspapers and farm journals, but he also owned a small library, which I still have, that included Richard Halliburton's *Royal Road to Romance,* a collection of A. Conan Doyle's Sherlock Holmes stories, and a complete set of Edgar Rice Burroughs's Tarzan books, each carefully signed and numbered by my father to indicate their proper sequence. By contrast, my mother read constantly and encouraged us children to do the same. Since we stayed busy most of the time, Mama and I always had a magazine or book to read while eating our meals, and this became a lifetime habit for my own family and me. The only exception was Sunday dinner, which had too formal an atmosphere for literature at the table. Sunday night, at suppertime, though, there was no such restraint.

Gloria remembered, "Mama always encouraged us to read. If we were reading, we didn't have to do any work, so we read a lot. I remember rainy afternoons with her, me, and Jimmy lying across the bed, reading. I'll tell you what kind of mother she was: I asked her to teach me how to play bridge. She handed me Ely Culbertson's book and said, 'Memorize this, and then you can play.'"

Daddy was the one who generally read to us when we were small children, as he sat in his easy chair in front of the fireplace with us on the floor in front of him. I remember Mama reading on some occasions from the Bible, usually with a concentration on the book of Ruth or Esther. Later in life, she never took any notable public positions on the liberation or equality of women but seemed to assume that any secondary or subservient role was the fault of the women involved. Her only departure from this general attitude was while she was in India in the Peace Corps, where she strongly condemned any kind of discrimination either against the lower castes of people or against wives or daughters within families.

Our house was located on the main highway and railroad running from Savannah on the Atlantic seacoast westward across Georgia and the continent. During some of the worst years of the Depression, the most frequent travelers we saw in front of our house were tramps, some looking out of open boxcar doors as the trains passed and a far greater number walking down the dirt road, in both directions. They were usually men traveling singly or in small groups, but every now and then an entire family would go by. Even as late as 1938, almost one-fourth of American workers were unemployed, and many came south for the warmer winters or just looking for employment.

When Mama was home, we never turned

away anyone who came to our house asking for food or a drink of water. They were invariably polite, and most of them offered to cut wood or do some other yard work in return for a sandwich or some leftover fried chicken or biscuits. We enjoyed talking to them and learned that many were relatively well educated and simply searching for odd jobs of any kind.

One day the lady from another farm on our road came to visit, and Mama commented on how many tramps she had helped that week. Mrs. Bacon said, "Well, I'm thankful that they never come in *my* yard."

The next time we had some of the vagrant visitors, Mama asked why they had stopped at our house and not the others. After some hesitation, one of them said, "Ma'am, we have a set of symbols that we use. The post on your mailbox is marked to say that you don't turn people away or mistreat us." After they were gone, we went out and found some unobtrusive scratches, and Mama told us not to change them.

Although a nurse, my mother was not immune to medical problems of her own. I first remember her as a very slender, almost gaunt, woman. There was a time when the doctors became concerned about her losing too much weight and prescribed iodized salt

Ruth, Lillian, Jimmy, 1934

(then not very common) for a goiter condition. I remember that she and Daddy joked about her also having to drink a bottle of beer each afternoon for medical reasons. Mama was pretty in her own way, with dark hair parted in the middle and eyes that always seemed to sparkle. At home, she wore loose-fitting dresses and was usually barefoot, and she seemed equally comfortable and at ease doing housework or lying on the couch reading a book. She slipped on soft canvas shoes before going out into the yard, because of the unavoidable droppings of chickens and other fowl. Mama seemed to me almost a different person, precise and businesslike, when she went on duty in her starched white nurse's dress and cap and white shoes, of which she was very proud.

My father's political beliefs were quite different from Mama's — at least compared with those she revealed after she became a widow. Daddy, along with almost everyone else in Georgia, voted for Franklin D. Roosevelt in 1932, but he was alienated by the New Deal programs that forced farmers to plow up their half-grown cotton, slaughter their growing pigs, and comply with strict acreage controls in order to qualify for government subsidy payments. For some, including my father, these were sacrilegious acts, and a totally unacceptable invasion by the federal government into the private affairs of free Americans. He was one of the few who, for the next three elections, voted for the national Republican ticket, while remaining a Democrat on the local and state races (there were no Republican candidates). I believe that he supported Harry Truman in 1948 (because I asked him to do so), but he never told me for sure. "Libertarian" would be my best description of his political philosophy.

One characteristic that Mama sometimes deplored but that I inherited from my father — reinforced by my years in the navy — was an obsession with punctuality. Daddy would always be well ahead of time to meet a train, attend a baseball game, or keep a personal appointment. It was inconceivable that his tardiness would keep anyone waiting, and he expected everyone around him to honor the same standards. When Daddy was scheduled for a physical examination of some kind, Mama would do everything possible both to remind him of the unpredictability of the medical profession and to encourage the doctor to be on time. She knew that if the physician was late, Daddy would look at his watch for a very few minutes and then leave. When Mama tried to chastise him, Daddy's reply was "I'm just as busy as he is."

In addition to nursing, Mama had pecans as a source of income. Based on a long-standing agreement between her and Daddy, all the pecan trees on our farm belonged to her, and during a couple of weeks late in November she arranged to remove her name from

Lillian and Earl Carter on a visit to submariner Jimmy and Rosalynn, San Diego, 1951

the nurses' call list so she could supervise the harvest. In the rare seasons when both the crop yield and prices were good, income from the nuts equaled what she earned all year from nursing. She spent this money as she saw fit, and it covered all the personal items we ordered from Sears, Roebuck and the clothing she bought at local stores for herself and my sisters.

Mama was thoroughly familiar with pecan culture and the characteristics of different varieties, and she consulted closely with the county agent on how to control the various diseases and insects. In November, armed with the longest bamboo poles she could find and with a cadre of hired women and boys, she made certain that every nut was knocked down, picked up, bagged, and then either polished in the hull or carefully shelled. Other farm boys and I climbed the trees to shake the limbs that the poles couldn't reach, and on a few occasions, Mama also climbed the trees. Gathering pecans, she always said, was "like picking up money off the ground."

Mother was a shrewd negotiator. Daddy never accompanied her when she drove our pickup truck, loaded with ten to twenty burlap bags of her nuts, each holding one hundred pounds, to Americus, but I went along whenever possible to watch the sale. I was always somewhat nervous but titillated by the pageant that was repeated during each visit. Mother's preferred market was in the busy store of Elias Attyah, a Lebanese American who knew more than anyone else in our region about this important crop. He supervised personally the purchase of each bagful of pecans, dumping them out into a

tilting wooden bin adjacent to the big over-
stuffed chair that accommodated his impos-
ing figure. He would scan the nuts, pick out
two or three, shell them, and examine the
kernels. When dealing with unsuspecting
or easily intimidated sellers who brought in
small lots from trees growing in their yards,
he would choose nuts whose inside kernels
he knew to be inferior, shake his head in dis-
appointment at what was revealed, and offer
a low price for the lot.

This didn't work with my mother. She
would watch impassively, then select a few
extra-good nuts from the bin and say, "Now
shell these!" Mr. Attyah would smile, look
at the superior kernels, and they would dis-
cuss the final price. Mama made a point
of knowing what all our Plains neighbors
had already received for their pecans, and
she invariably got the best prevailing prices.
She really liked Mr. Attyah, trusted him to
treat her fairly, and they both knew that all
Mama's pecans would come to him regardless of offers she received from other deal-
ers, who sometimes sent eager buyers to our
farm when the crop was short and demand
was high.

Even during the Depression years, Daddy,
Mama, Uncle Alton, and his wife, Annie

Laurie, saved enough money to take at least one trip each summer to Pittsburgh, Cincinnati, St. Louis, Chicago, Philadelphia, Boston, New York, or another major league city, usually in my uncle's Chrysler. They planned the trip for after crops were laid by and when they wouldn't miss our Baptist church revival, and so they could see the maximum number of baseball games, including at least one doubleheader. They continued these regular excursions for years after I left home, until Daddy was too sick to travel.

My parents had more flexibility in their schedule in those later years, and Mama always considered it to be one of God's special blessings that she and Daddy were present when Jackie Robinson played his first game for the Brooklyn Dodgers, in 1947. From then on, the Dodgers' general manager, Branch Rickey, was one of her special heroes because he brought Robinson to the major leagues, and she was a fervent Dodgers fan even after they moved to Los Angeles (and the Braves came to Atlanta). My mother watched or listened to every Dodgers game possible, and after our family became famous, she would call Tommy Lasorda to complain about managerial decisions he had made. When Mama died, we found a complete Dodgers uniform in her closet, even including cleats, with a love letter signed by the entire team.

Everyone knew that my daddy liked to have a good time, and my parents' companions on Saturday nights were quite often the local nurses and doctors. There was a group of five or six couples, whose leader was Dr. Sam Wise, the second of three brothers. Doctor Sam was single and was always dating the prettiest of the unmarried nurses. They sometimes rotated parties among the various homes, and I always dreaded my parents being hosts. They would push back the dining room table and chairs, use our small breakfast room as a bar, put us in bed early, and let their hair down. They must have thought that pulsating music, raucous laughter, and loud talking didn't penetrate our bedroom walls and doors. Doctor Sam had lost a leg during a childhood disease, and we could hear his special rhythm as our floors resounded with the loud taps of his wooden prosthesis. Sometimes the parties would last until it was almost time for Mama to fix breakfast and get the family off to church, where Daddy had to teach his regular Sunday School class.

When I was thirteen, Daddy built a fishpond and, overlooking it, the cabin known as the Pond House. It was about two miles from our home and became a favorite place for fishing, swimming, and entertaining friends. There was a pool table, a second-hand jukebox, and a large open room for dancing. Every now and then, one of the farmhands and I had to take a pair of mules over to the cabin the morning after one of my parents' parties to pull a guest's automobile out of the pond. The simple explanation was always "The brakes didn't hold." These guests were the gentry of the Plains community, who met to eat steak or fried chicken and to round-dance or Charleston to Victrola music. The men and women drank beer, wine, and bonded whiskey (bought from the local bootlegger, since ours was a dry county), and we children were always excluded from these events.

It was completely different when Mama and Daddy consorted with other farm families. They would take us children along, and the main dishes were usually barbecued pork and Brunswick stew. A few fiddlers played country music while one of them called big-circle square dances. Everybody drank sweet iced tea or lemonade with the meal, and between square dance sets the men passed around homemade moonshine in fruit jars, usually with Coca-Cola chasers. Honoring

the clearly understood proprieties, these refreshments would be shared out in the yard,
while a few of the women slipped a drink in
the kitchen. There were always discussions
about the quality of the 'shine, usually the
product of one of the dancers, just as a chef's
main course would be evaluated in a fancy
restaurant. Obviously, we children looked
forward to the farmers' dances, where the
smaller boys and girls were treated as though
we were invisible, teenagers were invited to
join the adult dancers, and the oldest boys
made something of a passage to adulthood
when finally permitted to have a toddy with
the adults.

Despite his political aversion to FDR and
the New Deal, Daddy became a leader in
the program that brought electric power
to our area and other rural communities
in 1938. Two years later, he didn't object
when I took a government job. I earned a
monthly paycheck by measuring the acreage
of fields to ensure compliance with restric-
tive allotments for cotton and peanuts. The
pay was twenty-eight cents an hour with my
furnishing transportation, and I would have
lost money if Mama had not been staying at
home with Billy, then a baby, allowing me
to use the family's 1937 Plymouth without
charge.

5
THE PRACTICE OF MEDICINE

My mother was one of about two dozen nurses who practiced their profession in and around the town of Plains. Her first preference was being in charge of the operating room, but this was a high privilege she could not retain when her rigid nursing schedule was interrupted by a growing family. Private duty in the hospital was her next choice — twelve hours a day, for which the Wise brothers paid her four dollars. After a few years of this, as Daddy's income increased and when none of our family required her close attention, Mama decided to shift to private duty in people's homes. This gave her more flexibility and independence, but there were two problems: the time required was twenty hours per day, and the six dollars' pay was the responsibility of the patient. Payment was a doubtful prospect indeed during the days of the Great Depression.

In many cases, families had little if any

contact with a medical doctor, so my mother both provided medical care and served as a diagnostician. Her relationship with Dr. Sam Wise was especially close. She consulted with him on doubtful cases, and he sometimes wrote prescriptions based on Mama's assessment of a case. It was understood that payment for her services would be made during the fall harvest season or whenever funds or farm produce (usually chickens, eggs, blackberries, chestnuts, or hogs) became available. One memorable payment was a wagonload of turpentine chips, hauled to our house from more than twenty-five miles away, which would become instantly aflame and were invaluable in starting fires on cold mornings. In more cases than were ever mentioned until after his death, Daddy provided money to Mama for buying needed medicines, and she waived payment for nursing.

There were about two hundred black people living in the Archery community, owning their own farms, working for the railroad, sharecropping, or doing day labor. None of them owned an automobile, so they had to walk to town or perhaps ride in a wagon. Treatment in a hospital was for the wealthy or for especially difficult special cases. Mama was glad to receive some compensation in the early years, but she said, "After Earl told me we didn't really need the money any longer, I quit charging anything for my nursing duty, except in the hospital."

On my bookshelf I have a copy of the 1921 *Lippincott's Nursing Manual,* which Mama had used to prepare for her state board examination and which served in later years as a handy reference guide. Her pride in it was indicated by her signature, "Miss Lillian Gordy," inscribed in nine places, often followed by "Wise Sanitarium, Plains, Ga." On the preface page are listed the "1922 girls in training," with "Miss" preceding the last names of twenty-three young women, plus one preceded by a "Mrs." I still remember many of them: Miss Webb, Miss Arrington, Miss Pennington, and Mrs. Abrams. For the rest of their lives, they called each other either by their first names or Webb, Arrington, and Gordy, reflecting their strong and permanent sense of sorority.

Most of the manual describes the regular duties of a nurse, with special attention to the use of Latin words and abbreviations and the translation of doctors' prescriptions. There is a fairly thorough presentation of symptoms and standard treatments for the common ailments of the time, most of them now of concern only to people in Africa and a few other places in the Third World, and some then-fatal infections, like streptococci. For some reason, the entry on syphilis is heavily underlined.

I particularly enjoyed reading the section titled "Nursing Ethics." With one exception, the nurse is expected to treat the attending physician with the utmost respect, almost reverence. There is no advice on how to respond to improper personal advances by a doctor, presumably because such a perfect person should never be criticized. The exception was if called on a case by a doctor who was known to have performed an abortion. The advice is to refuse, "for you could not afford to associate in private nursing with a criminal or a malefactor of this type."

I notice that the corners of some pages are still turned down. One of them is a description of how a nurse could "ethically" give a discount for her services to a poor family without embarrassing them. There is a sample bill, which shows a standard charge of twenty-eight dollars a week, in this case eighty dollars for twenty days, but with a discount, called an "allowance," to pay for the nurse's pleasure derived from living in the patient's home. If there were small children there, "the nurse should take the place of the mother, provided she does not have to neglect the patient."

Despite the lectures in school and from my mother about malaria, various fevers, and other vector-borne diseases, there was not really much that we children could do about the ubiquitous insects and rodents. As far as flies and mosquitoes were concerned, our screen doors were opened too many times each day to keep them out of our house. Any container of milk or other food had to be kept covered, often with a piece of cheese-cloth. We used flyswatters and sticky tapes hanging from the ceiling to reduce the insect population, but there was always a fresh phalanx waiting outside the back door — and new ones breeding on feces in the surrounding yard and nearby barn lot. The old joke was that cooking chitterlings (pig intestines) was the only thing that would make the flies find ways to get *out* of a house.

The many areas around and under the nearby outbuildings were inhabited by enormous wharf rats, who nested in labyrinths of tunnels even beneath concrete floors and could successfully challenge most cats. The only counteractions available in those days were strychnine (which also killed other animals) and rat terrier dogs, which were owned and handled by professionals who contracted for their services. Smaller mice were everywhere, too numerous to be controlled.

This was, therefore, a time of typhus, scarlet and typhoid fevers, diphtheria, and deadly cases of tetanus (lockjaw), influenza, and pneumonia; chronic cases of tapeworm, hookworm, pellagra, trachoma, malaria, mumps, whooping cough, measles, chicken pox, and polio. Treatment was with aspirin, milk of magnesia, castor oil, 666 Cold Preparation, quinine, paregoric, Mercurochrome, iodine, and various patent medicines that were primarily alcohol and sometimes opium. As an avid bottle collector, I cherish a small bottle found in the woods near Plains, embossed with the words ELIXIR OF OPIUM. There were no effective antibiotics such as penicillin, and a serious infection was often fatal. My uncle Alton's wife, Annie Laurie, died with a strep throat.

It seemed that none of the treatments for our ailments were pleasant. We always suspected that the patent medicine manufacturers had concluded that only evil tastes and smells were effective in combating germs — or perhaps they were simply responding to their customers' beliefs. Castor oil, 666 Cold

Preparation, and paregoric all met the test, and hot poultices and iodine burned enough to be respected on croupy chests and open cuts and scratches. I think the most obnoxious medical experience I ever had was when someone convinced Daddy that we children could avoid an outbreak of flu or some other prevalent illness by wearing pellets of asafetida, or devil's dung, in belts around our waists. It was a horrible-smelling extract from some kind of root and undoubtedly derived its protective reputation by keeping bearers of germs at a healthy distance from the wearers of the stench. We wore it until we all convinced Daddy that the threat had passed.

Thanks to our short hair, one common affliction that we boys usually avoided was head lice, but even with the good hygiene that Mama enforced around our house, both my sisters had this problem on occasion. Other than a very short haircut or shaved head, the standard treatment was a concoction of sulfur and kerosene, held in place with a tight stocking cap. Whenever we saw a schoolmate wearing a hat all during the day, we knew what her problem was.

We didn't worry much about red bugs, or chiggers, but Mama made us check for ticks after we'd spent time in the woods and swamps. She knew how to remove them with heat or tweezers, so the aftermath of their bites was never serious for us more fortunate children.

Others were not so fortunate. A study of black and white rural schoolchildren during the 1930s revealed hookworm infection rates of 50 percent in some areas. The difference between me and some of my playmates was that Mama always put medicine on infected places, which prevented the parasites from migrating over time into my lungs, then throat, and from there into the small intestine. Untreated, the millions of tiny worms consumed a major portion of the scarce nutrients within the bodies of our poorest neighbors. More significantly, I guess, we avoided hookworm by having a fairly sanitary outdoor toilet and not habitually walking in soil that included human excrement. Also, after 1935 we had running water in our home and could bathe more frequently.

Any serious illness involved the entire community. When one child came down with polio, our school would close for a few days, and all of us began to imagine the symptoms: fatigue, headaches, fever, and a stiff neck. No matter how serious the disease, the patient would almost invariably stay at home, and not in the hospital. When a serious illness occurred, the family's home would be surrounded by vehicles of all kinds, as the house and yard filled with neighbors come to share the grief, bring food, assist in care, or join in prayers for recovery. In illnesses like double pneumonia, there seemed always to be a crisis, a point at which the patient would either die or take a turn for the better. In either case, the news brought to the door by a doctor or nurse would almost instantly sweep the town.

Wise Sanitarium was widely known for its advanced use of anesthesia, surgery, and radium treatment. The eldest doctor, Thad Wise, was also an expert on nutrition, having recognized that many of the prevailing diseases were caused by inadequate diets. He knew that sweet potatoes provide a number of vitamins and other nutrients absent from habitual meals of grits, corn bread, and fatback, and Daddy responded to Mama's request to plant each year a large field of sweet potatoes, which were distributed without cost to any of our neighbors who came to harvest them.

Many children died with colitis in those days. For a near-fatal attack when I was four years old, my mother followed a long series of unsuccessful treatments with an ultimate suggestion by a country doctor from nearby Montezuma. The therapy involved a saturated solution of cornstarch administered as an enema. "And in two weeks he was completely healed," she declared. "Later, after we were so successful with Jimmy, whenever a child — black or white — had colitis, the doctors in Plains would call me and say, 'Would you show the parents what to do?' The treatment, although unpleasant, was the greatest thing that ever happened."

The highest social and financial distinction around Plains was to be a medical doctor, and particularly one who practiced in the Wise Sanitarium. These men enjoyed extraordinary respect, almost as if they were superhuman. In a time when so many diseases threatened to be fatal, it seemed that our very lives were constantly in their hands, and we appreciated their skills and the terrible burden of their work. They were always on call, either within the hospital or, more often, to attend patients in their homes. Every citizen of Plains was a walking advertisement for the hospital's high quality of health care and loved to repeat what may have been folktales about the institution. We were convinced that our hospital was the best, even compared with the much larger and more famous ones in

Atlanta and farther north.

I and the other older citizens of Plains can still name the young medical interns who went on to greater things, including an anesthesiologist who earned a national reputation with innovative techniques, a famous ophthalmologist in Columbus, and the chief surgeon at Emory University Hospital in Atlanta. Just as fine, in our opinion, was the training program for registered nurses. Although they were highly disciplined and reduced to virtual peonage within the hospital environment, they were the objects of admiration and some jealousy among the citizens of our town. There was no higher calling for a woman than to become a nurse, especially one trained at Wise Sanitarium. There is no doubt that these opinions were influenced by the nurse graduates who became the wives of fortunate young men and the mothers of a number of my schoolmates and me.

Physicians were immune to disparaging gossip, although it was generally known, at least in our family, which doctors and nurses were "living in sin." This phrase did not have such a negative connotation when applied to the doctors, as most people seemed to feel that dedicated physicians had a right to enjoy the few hours they were off duty, and the community did not condemn their sexual peccadilloes. Everyone accepted the fact that Gussie Abrams, my godmother, lived with Dr. Thad Wise, who was a widower. I became at least indirectly involved in this love affair when Mrs. Abrams got pregnant and bore a son, who was named for me. Little Jimmy died after only a few weeks, however, and was buried in the family cemetery of her husband, with whom Gussie had not lived for several years.

Until I went away to college, no one in Plains had ever been divorced; divorce was considered to be a sin against God committed only in Hollywood and among some of the more irresponsible New Yorkers. The oath given during the marriage ceremony was regarded as inviolable, based on the words of Christ himself, who, when questioned about marriage, referred to the first binding of Adam and Eve, concluding with "Therefore what God has joined together, let no man put asunder."

For some reason, this commandment was considered to have priority over the one against adultery. One of the most notable cases involved two white families who lived in a fairly remote area near Archery. In what was obviously a totally harmonious arrangement, the two husbands simply swapped wives and a total of nine children. Perhaps to minimize false rumors, one of the husbands came over to our house and described their decision to my father. Other children were born to the new couples, and the resulting common-law marriages remained intact thereafter, but the parents stopped going to church.

The effect of Mother's nursing on other people was memorable as a childhood fact of life, and it also affected our relationships. When she was on twenty-hour duty, we small children were given adequate care by at least one of the black women who lived nearby. We were expected to perform our share of the chores around the house, like sweeping the yards; feeding the large flock of chickens, ducks, and guinea fowl; collecting eggs; and toting in wood for the kitchen stove. We never saw Mama when her four hours off duty were around midnight, but she would leave her instructions for us on a black desk in the front room. Much later, we would tease her by claiming that we thought the black desk was our mother.

When questioned later by a news reporter about having left Daddy and us children to nurse others, she responded, "I do believe in working women and I feel so strongly that a child is better off not to have the mother every minute of the time. Children who cling to their mothers grow up being babies."

Because of Mama's profession, the nurses and doctors in our hospital helped to shape my life's interest in medicine — or at least the preventive aspect. My earliest memories of Wise Sanitarium are of the occasions when Mother would let me cross the road from the schoolhouse to eat a hot meal with the nurses when she was on duty and not at home to fix my lunch. I didn't realize then what a treasure we had in Plains — a truly outstanding medical center with all the economic and scientific benefits that it brought to the community. Compared with those in other small rural towns, the interests of our citizens were expanded by the stream of doctors and nurses who came to live among us as they trained or practiced their profession.

Because I was "Miss Gordy's little boy" and a pet of the nurses, my life was especially blessed. The senior nurse, Mrs. Abrams, was my godmother, and she had high expectations for me. On my eighth birthday she gave me a leather-bound collection of Victor Hugo's works and a twenty-volume set of The Outline of Knowledge. This is still one of my treasured possessions.

When Mama was not nursing, she was in charge of the house. She was up before first light to fix breakfast for us, usually after my father had already gone to the barn or fields to get all the farming tasks under way. On school days she would get us all fed, dressed, and on the way with lunch in a paper sack or one-gallon lard bucket. Summertime was much more pleasant; I would often go early to the field with Daddy, and if it was near home, we might come in later in the morning for breakfast. Mama usually had some help with heavy cleaning, and she sent our dirty clothes off in a long square-bottomed white oak basket to be washed each week by a black family near Plains who provided this service for the community.

Relieved of most household duties, my mother was free to pursue her chosen profession — both in these early years and for three more decades.

6
DEALING WITH
THE RACE ISSUE

Without any fanfare, Mother just ignored the pervasive restraints of racial segregation. It should be remembered that in those days so-called "separate but equal" was the law of the land — ordained by the U.S. Supreme Court and strongly enforced by all local authorities in the South and much of the North. The racial separation applied to schools, churches, transportation, and access to the systems of politics and justice. Where we lived, black citizens had their own (inferior) public schools, attended their own (superior) churches, and did not have the right to become registered voters or to cast a ballot — certainly not to hold public office. They did not serve on juries, and their proper place in courtrooms was in a balcony, a remote corner, or as the accused.

There were no civil rights lawyers or enlightened religious leaders demanding that the separate but equal system be changed.

My first acquaintance with racial equality came much later, in 1945, when a black student, Wesley Brown, was permitted to join us in the ranks of midshipmen at the U.S. Naval Academy. Three years later, while I was serving as a submarine officer, President Harry Truman ordained that all military services be integrated. This was more than seven years before Rosa Parks insisted on sitting in the front of a Montgomery bus, or before Martin Luther King, Jr., became famous.

In the rural community of Archery, we children were raised intimately with our black peers. All of my playmates were black, and I was absorbed in their culture — except when I went, somewhat reluctantly, to school or church. We played, wrestled, fought, went fishing and hunting, and worked in the fields together — as equals. When my parents were away, I slept in the home of Rachel and Jack Clark, an admirable black couple who nurtured me and introduced me to many aspects of life. In my book about our childhood, *An Hour Before Daylight,* I concluded that, in addition to my parents, only two of the five people who shaped my life were white. My mother was the only white adult I ever knew who had a similarly equal relationship with our neighbors.

Other white people's response to Mama's actions was either to ignore them or to make excuses that she was a member of the medical community and therefore obligated to treat both races the same, at least when she was on duty. An additional factor was that my father's growing prestige and influence in the community made our family somewhat immune to social ostracism or punishment.

Mama was one of the strong, able, and independent Southern women who became a powerful societal force during the generation or two after the War Between the States because of what had happened to the men and boys. Many were dead or incapacitated, or were rendered ignoble by their military defeat and the loss of their prestige, property, and political rights during the imposition of the carpetbagger governments. Every community knew these matriarchs, who were envied and sometimes despised because of their eccentricities, but always respected. It seems to me that the South has a tradition of accommodating eccentrics, as long as they are self-confident, strong enough, or immune to social ostracism.

The richest and most famous man in the Archery community was African Methodist

Episcopal Bishop William Dexter Johnson. He was the leader of black Methodists in five upper Midwest states and an international traveler. He was also a personal friend of my grandfather Jim Jack Gordy. By law, he had to comply with some aspects of segregation, but he was able to ignore those that were imposed by custom. One of these was that a black person didn't approach the front door of a white family's house but always came to the back. When Bishop Johnson wanted to speak to my father, he would send his chauffeur first to make an appointment, and at the scheduled time his large black Cadillac or Packard would pull into our front yard and the chauffeur would sound the horn. Daddy would then go out for the desired conversation.

One of the bishop's children was Alvan, who was a student at Harvard and especially close to my mother. He paid no attention to the back door rule and would knock on the front door when he wanted to see Mama. My recollection (with which my mother later disagreed) is that Daddy, if at home, would remain in the back rooms or go down to the barn until this impropriety was terminated — but he was never known to question my mother's decisions concerning race.

Willis Wright was the preeminent sharecropper who lived on our farm in Webster County, a leader among his peers and highly respected by everyone who knew him. He was a special friend of my mother's, primarily because of a serious ailment involving his kidneys. Willis would never come to our commissary or visit families on the home place without coming by for a conversation with Mama. Eventually, he had to have surgery at Wise Sanitarium to remove one of his kidneys, while Mama served as the nurse in charge of the operating room. During Willis's long recuperation at home, Daddy would take Mama to see him on Daddy's routine visits to the farm.

I remember how surprised and disconcerted we were when around harvest time one year Willis Wright proposed that he buy the farm on which he lived. It was a reasonable request but a startling one, impossible to grant. Although Daddy had bought and sold a number of tracts of farmland around the general community, this place was special. Its 215 acres lay in the heart of our original family property. In fact, some of Daddy's siblings still owned an interest in the land. Since Daddy and Willis were very close friends, the obvious solution was for Daddy to help Willis locate another small farm that was on the market.

One day during the next Christmas holi-days, Daddy asked Mama and me to go with him to Webster County, and we drove directly to the house where Willis lived. When we arrived, we sat on the porch for a while, talking about his good crop that year, the state of his health, and plans for the next planting season. At a pause in the conversation, I could see that my father was struggling with his emotions. Finally, he blurted out, "Willis, I've decided to sell you the farm." This was a surprise to all of us. Mama burst into tears of joy and put her arms around my father.

After the general commotion died down, Daddy told Willis to come to the store the following Saturday, when they would work out the terms of the sale. Before another year went by, there was a new concrete-block home on the site, painted green, and with Daddy's help, the rural electrification agency made it the first house in the area to be wired for electricity, early in the 1940s.

With news reporters, Mama was always pro-tective of my father's reputation regarding race. This is one of her typical statements when the media began to probe our family's history:

"One thing bothers me. You reporters

Earl Carter as a state legislator, 1953

have criticized my husband lately about not being for racial integration. What you don't recognize is that he died when there was no such thing as integration and nobody had ever heard of Martin Luther King or any civil rights movement. Earl always rejected all the racist organizations that degraded or persecuted black people, and both races always knew this to be true. I was real controversial in the community sometimes, but he supported everything I did to help black people and always went out of his way to treat all people with complete respect and to deal with them honestly and fairly." She was right, of course.

Daddy was serving his first term as a state legislator in 1953 when we learned that he was terminally ill with pancreatic cancer. I had pressing duties helping to build a pioneer nuclear power plant for submarines and was working in Schenectady, New York, for Admiral Hyman Rickover and taking advanced nuclear studies at Union College. I requested two weeks of leave time and drove to Plains in July to be at Daddy's bedside during his final days. Except for very brief periods while on annual leave from the U.S. Navy, I had not been at home during the previous ten years.

As mentioned earlier, President Truman had integrated the military service, but I expected to face some different and unpleasant circumstances in the still legally segregated South. I was surprised to welcome to my parents' home a stream of white and black visitors, bringing flowers, fruit, vegetables, cakes, pies, and other choice prepared foods. Daddy was far too ill to receive any visitors, and I had the responsibility of extended conversations with the well-wishers. I was both amazed and overwhelmed by the broad range of his interests, the expressed affection for my father, and numerous accounts of his previously unrevealed acts of generosity and kindness.

My father took his last terrible breath in the arms of Annie Mae Hollis, a black woman who had helped our family on the Archery farm. She had been working with the wealthy Chasen family, which owned one of Hollywood's most famous restaurants, but came back to Plains when she heard of Daddy's illness.

These few days of unexpected revelations literally changed my life. I had come home with no thought of interrupting what was an enjoyable and quite successful naval career. I really struggled against the thought of relinquishing what had been my life's dream since I was a little child, but I began to assess the breadth of my father's activities and his beneficial influence in this small rural community. As I drove back toward Schenectady, where Rosalynn and our three sons were waiting for me to resume my duties, I became convinced that I should resign from the navy and return to a totally unpredictable life as a farmer in Plains.

Rosalynn was horrified by my decision and objected strenuously. I remember that, three months later, she hardly spoke to me as we drove home, and there was a chill between us for weeks after we moved into a tiny apartment in a government housing project. Her concerns seemed to be justified when our total income in 1954 was less than three hundred dollars.

Without any indication that I might actually be at home more than a few days after his death, Daddy had designated his only brother, Alton, as the executor of his will. Alton (whom we called Uncle Buddy) very quickly assigned me all the responsibilities, which afflicted me with a crash course in the affairs of our farms and the agricultural supply business. They turned out to be quite complex, but I was able to resolve all the financial issues through the 1953 harvest season and then divide the estate into five parts — as equally as I could. During one brief session at my parents' home in Plains, I showed the maps and documents to everyone and then, beginning with the youngest, let Billy, Ruth, Gloria, and Mama make their choices. I took what was left and started the life of a farmer and small-town warehouseman with Mother as my partner.

Mama had rejected a unanimous proposal

by local political leaders to accept Daddy's seat in the state legislature and seemed to be not only grief-stricken but withdrawn and bitter. We hoped that her financial interest in the family business and becoming the "mother hen" of a larger brood of grandchildren would boost her spirits.

7
NEW INTERESTS AS A WIDOW

To us children, it appeared that our mother had two different characters: before and after her husband's death. There was no doubt among all those who knew her that, as a widow, Mother blossomed forth in many ways and increasingly seemed to be searching for whatever was provocative, adventurous, challenging, and gratifying. Daddy had seemed to make the final decisions about family matters when we were growing up. We could see that there was an unspoken but clear division of responsibilities in the family; anything inside the house was Mama's, plus all the affairs of my two sisters, including selecting and buying clothing for her and them. Her medical career was always exclusively hers, including the periods when she chose to be on call for duty, but during later years she would sometimes use the excuse "Earl doesn't want me to work right now."

Now, with her husband gone, my mother

strongly asserted her claim to be the matriarch of our family, around whom the lives of all her children and grandchildren revolved. She was overly generous in trying to meet our sometimes conflicting needs, but she expected in return that all of us would give top priority to her proper treatment. She was quite harsh in her criticism when any of us failed to make a regular pilgrimage to pay our respects. This was never an unpleasant burden, because our visits with her were filled with interesting conversation and provocative arguments. She monitored a wide range of sporting events closely and remained abreast of the latest news. During the last quarter century of her life, she was intensely interested in national political affairs and a strong supporter of Democratic candidates — usually those who were the most fervently committed to civil rights at home and human rights around the world.

My most vivid memory of Mother during my early days back home was her watching the Joseph McCarthy hearings for the entire thirty-six days in 1954. I don't think she ever missed a moment of the television drama, and she urged me to join her whenever I could. She despised McCarthy, and was overjoyed when the U.S. Senate subsequently censured him.

After Mama had stayed at home for a few months, she talked to her older sister, Susie, who was the housemother for a fraternity at Auburn University, and decided to take a similar position caring for about a hundred Kappa Alphas. This is a fraternal order founded in 1865 that is heavily concentrated in the South, largely based on a reverence for General Robert E. Lee. At least at Auburn, the fraternity had the reputation — which they nurtured carefully — of being the most rambunctious on the campus, raising hell whenever possible and with members often in trouble with the university's administrators.

That suited Mama perfectly, and she was soon deeply immersed in the KAs' fraternal and personal affairs. She bought a new Cadillac every couple of years and took it to Auburn to be used as a free limousine for her boys. She served as a banker and something of a priest for those in trouble with finances or in their love affairs, and she was proud to be their confidante when problems were too sensitive or embarrassing to be shared with their own parents. She was always available to help them and couldn't go to sleep until the last ones were back in their rooms or had let her know where they were.

A few times during her eight years at Auburn, Mama asked Rosalynn and me to join her as official chaperones when the fraternity went to Panama City on the nearby Gulf Coast. She gave us quiet instructions, primarily of caution about not interfering too much in the right of the boys and their dates to enjoy themselves. Excessive public drunkenness and violence leading to bloodshed were about the only things that were out of bounds. We were present just to fill some kind of student-to-chaperone ratio established by the university. At least we also enjoyed the free vacations.

It eventually became obvious to Gloria and me that Mama's strenuous life was taking an excessive toll on her financial and physical well-being, and eventually, after Aunt Susie retired, we were able to induce our mother to return to Plains. Throughout the rest of her life, a stream of KA alumni came by her home in Plains to pay their respects and reminisce about past escapades.

Before my father's death, we had never had any indication that Mama's secret ballot in an election might have canceled Daddy's vote. Now, back at home and with more time to spare, she became quite active in supporting national Democratic candidates. She was stricken with grief when John Kennedy was assassinated and publicly castigated the racial conservatives around Plains who applauded his death. As the new president, Lyndon Johnson made it clear that he would go far beyond anything the Kennedys had attempted in bringing an end to legal racial segregation. This was an extremely unpopular position throughout our region, as Johnson well understood, so he ostentatiously wrote off the states in the Deep South and avoided campaigning during 1964 in Georgia, Alabama, Mississippi, or Louisiana.

My mother committed herself totally to the Democratic presidential campaign that year and volunteered to head the Johnson-Humphrey organization in Sumter County. Although few white people let such a choice be known, our entire family supported her efforts, and our sons in high school were ridiculed and abused by their schoolmates. Chip came home one day crying, with a bloody nose and his shirt ripped. He had had a fistfight when someone pulled a chair from behind him at choir practice, causing him to sprawl on the floor. He declared, "I'm never going to be a Democrat again, or put another Johnson sticker on my notebook!" But he was back at school the next morning with a fresh decal, still a Democrat.

Much later, in a 1976 *Redbook* interview, Mama said, "People hated Johnson down here because of his stand on civil rights and it got very ugly, but I was never afraid, not even when they threw things at my car and yelled, 'Nigger lover, nigger lover' at me." Almost every day, her Cadillac, parked in front of Johnson's county headquarters in the old Windsor Hotel, would be covered with abusive graffiti, several times with the radio antenna broken off or tied in a knot.

Lady Bird Johnson and Vice President Hubert Humphrey and his wife, Muriel, did come to Georgia during the '64 campaign, and my mother worked with them and a few of Johnson's cabinet members. On one occasion, the Humphreys arranged to go to Moultrie for a Democratic rally, and Mama and my sister Gloria were given the honor of meeting them at the airport and driving them into the South Georgia town. Senator Humphrey made the main speech, and a luncheon was planned for his wife and a large group of local women.

Gloria was driving toward the hotel where the luncheon would be served when Mrs. Humphrey asked, "Are any black women invited to the event?" For a long time no one spoke, and finally my sister said, "I don't know." She knew quite well that there weren't. Muriel said, "If not, then I'm not going in." They stopped the car in front of the hotel, and Mama went inside to relay their guest's decision to the hostess. She came back in a few minutes and said, "Muriel, everything's okay." So they all went in, and, sure enough, there were several black ladies present. In fact, they were among the first to greet the honored guest, who never knew that the hotel maids just took off their aprons for the occasion. That was the first racially integrated social affair in South Georgia, and the credit should go to Muriel Humphrey — and my mother.

Mama was a delegate to the Democratic Party Convention that year in Atlantic City, and she was overwhelmed when she had a chance to meet Bobby Kennedy after he made a memorable speech about his brother.*

Within a few days after the convention in Atlantic City, my mother learned that her friends Pete and Dot Godwin were planning

* Despite her admiration for Hubert Humphrey, I learned that Mama would be supporting Kennedy in 1968 as the next president. I had not made a choice among the contenders for the Democratic nomination, but Bobby told some of his young Georgia campaign workers that he had a strong supporter in the Carter family.

to open a small nursing home in Blakely, about sixty miles southwest of Plains. Pete was our town's druggist, and Dot was a registered nurse and the manager of a nursing home housed in the old Wise Sanitarium facilities. Dot came to see Mama and asked if she would help them get the new place organized. Mama talked to me and Gloria about the proposal, saying that there would be only thirty patients, that she still had her nursing license but needed to upgrade her service record, and that she might go down there for a week or two just to help recruit a nursing staff and a permanent manager. Besides, she was bored!

Mama later described this experience: "To my surprise, I finally stayed for eighteen months, and turned out to be the administrator as well as head nurse. I did everything, from buying beds and bedpans to making sure the heat and air-conditioning worked. I hired all the workers and managed in a short time to get the place fully certified. I devised my own formula for running a successful nursing home. It was my decision to hire two registered nurses and one licensed practical nurse to take over eight-hour shifts. The LPN was on duty the same time I was. Medication could be given only by registered nurses, so when the LPN was there, I gave the medication myself. You can understand why I couldn't get back home very often."

One of Mama's most innovative and controversial policies was that any person bringing a patient for admission to the nursing home had to sign an agreement for a close family member to visit at least once a week. Mama added, "It was a good idea and only failed one time, when the sister of a patient did not come to visit her for two weeks. I called the woman and told her that I had ordered an ambulance that would be bringing her sister home to live with her. 'Oh my God, please don't!' the woman replied. 'I'll be there in an hour to see her.' I scared her to death, and never had any more trouble."

I talked to Dot Godwin recently, and she said, "Lilly was a damn good nurse and manager, but pitiful as a bookkeeper. One of her habits that cost us a lot of money was a requirement that every sheet had to be changed each day. She explained that she had always done that in her own house. We could tell that she was getting tired of the job, and being away from home, when she began to complain that most of the patients were younger than she was. Not long after that she located a permanent manager that was okay with me and Pete, and she came back to Plains.

"She had great rapport with black people, all of whom seemed to trust her. I remember that one day a young boy climbed up on top of the Plains water tank and announced that he was going to kill himself. He rejected all the efforts of people to talk to him and declared that he would jump if anybody tried to climb up the ladder. Finally, someone said, 'Why don't we go and get Miss Lillian?'

"When Lilly got there, she told all the other folks to back away, and she and the boy began to shout back and forth. She soon found out that the boy's stepfather had been whipping him and he had decided to end his life. Lilly finally told him, 'I'm coming up there with you,' and she climbed up that little rickety ladder about a hundred feet off the ground.

"After a little while, Lilly called for the sheriff to come close, and asked him if he could prevent any further beatings. When she and the sheriff promised to go to the boy's home and work out the problem, Lilly and the boy came back down to the ground. I don't think anybody else could have done what she did. When people would mention it later, she said, 'It wasn't much higher than some of my pecan trees, and I just asked the boy what he wanted.'"

Dot also commented about Mama's being

a member of the fairly exclusive Stitch and Chat Club in Plains but always refusing to bring anything to sew. It was mostly a social gathering with conversation — sometimes heated — as the main attraction. "Lilly would try to settle arguments, but she used the occasions to learn what anyone might be needing and then would quietly take care of it."

8

AN ELDERLY PEACE CORPS VOLUNTEER

One night, early in 1966, my mother saw a
television advertisement for Peace Corps volunteers with the slogan "Age is no barrier."
She immediately sent a letter volunteering
to serve but had second thoughts the next
day. She came down to the warehouse where
Billy and I were working, certain, she later
said, that we would talk her out of her plan.
Her first question to us was "Do y'all love
me?" I responded, "Mama, you know that
we love you." Billy's was more prescient:
"Mama, what the hell are you gonna do
now?" We were soon giving her encourage-
ment to go ahead with her plans, and Gloria
and Ruth were not inclined to discourage
her either. She said, "Even though I felt that
they were just trying to get rid of me for two
years, I had to follow through in order not
to lose face with my children and the rest of
the family."

She soon filled out the official documents

describing her qualifications and reasons for wishing to serve. Her only request was to be sent "where it's warm, people have dark skins, and need a nurse's service." (She was posted to India.)

During the two years my mother was in the Peace Corps, she wrote letters home at least every week, and my sister Gloria collected them from all of us children. They were later collated and slightly edited by Gloria and Mama, and published by Simon & Schuster in 1977 as *Away from Home: Letters to My Family.* Although long out of print, the book is being reissued this year, so I have decided to minimize my quotations from the text.

However, I discovered an additional source of information about Mother's experiences in a small diary, which she had given to her youngest sister and was later donated to my presidential library. This is my primary source for the text that follows.

I was running for governor of Georgia at the time — a last-minute shift I made after withdrawing from a race for the U.S. Congress that I had already won. Mama was deeply involved in the gubernatorial campaign, and despite our urging, she refused to stop and go shopping for what she might need in

India. She insisted that she would just carry a few things she already owned. She did finally take one day off to buy some special items, mostly paperback books, cosmetics, and underwear.

We drove Mama to Atlanta on September 10, 1966, leaving her house in Plains unlocked for the duration of her absence, so all the family could use it as needed. She took a plane to Chicago, where she spent three months at the University of Chicago for preliminary language training and for psychiatric and other tests to assure that she was qualified for two years of strenuous duty at a not yet disclosed place in India. Her diary shows that she was desperately afraid of being "deselected" because of her excessive eagerness to please everyone, her increasingly revealed lack of competence in learning the assigned Marathi dialect, and especially her age.

One of her first crises was bumping her leg on a chair in her hotel room and then falling down. She didn't dare tell anyone, but her knee swelled so much that she was unable to walk. Instead of claiming illness, she called and volunteered to do typing rather than hand out birth control pamphlets on the Chicago streets.

"They asked me if I could type, and I said 'yes.' After they brought a typewriter and a lot of envelopes and addresses to my room, I locked the door and looked at the typewriter — then I looked out the window to see how far it was to the ground. (I didn't want to mess myself up too bad if I decided to jump.) I finally figured out how to put the paper in, and after fooling with it thirty minutes, mashed the right button to make a capital letter. It took me more time to find that long thing on the bottom that made the space between words. It took me all day to address forty envelopes, and I'm afraid they'll think I did such a good job they might ask me to do this every time. Lord, won't I ever learn to say 'No'?"

The psychiatrist came to join the group twice a week and seemed to take a special interest in my mother. He persisted in asking her to explain why a well-off Southern widow, whose son was a state senator and running for governor, was volunteering to serve dark-skinned people in the stifling Indian heat. Her medical files subsequently revealed that he concluded she was exorcising her demons of white guilt over Southern race relations.

Mama survived all her early tests, and in mid-December, she and thirty-six other vol-

Lillian as Peace Corps volunteer, en route to India, 1966

unteers flew to New Delhi, with stops in Atlanta, London, Rome, and Beirut — where, she wrote, "Intrigue, etc. filled the air."

The first assignment for the group was to go to the American embassy in New Delhi, where Ambassador Chester Bowles gave what Mother called "the dullest talk I ever heard," and she went sound asleep. During the next ten days the volunteers learned more about India and its needs, and Mother was informed that her primary duty would be helping to implement Prime Minister Indira Gandhi's family planning program. As a registered nurse, Mother would be responsible for educating the families on birth control measures, including the insertion of "loops" (intrauterine contraceptive devices) into women and encouraging the men to have vasectomies. She would then assist doctors in the simple surgery that would end pregnancies in the families. Her duty assignment would be near Bombay, in a community named Vikhroli, an industrial complex comprising seven factories and about twenty thousand people. It was owned — and totally controlled — by the wealthy and influential Godrej family.

Mother and another elderly lady, named Mabel Yewell, were assigned a small but comfortable apartment among a few more privileged employees. Across the valley they could see the mud-and-grass huts of the families with whom they would be working. There were two clinics, one for general medical treatment of the working families and the other for surgeries, plus medical care for supervisory personnel.

In the relatively controlled environment

of the Godrej complex, Prime Minister Gandhi wanted to limit family size to a maximum of two children, or just one if it were a boy. Violation of this threshold could result in a limit on social services, housing choices, public education, and opportunities for job advancement. Mama wrote that Mrs. Godrej invited a famous gynecologist, Dr. Soonawalla, to meet the surgeons who performed the vasectomies. He was known for having invented a newer, cheaper contraceptive loop for women's use.

One problem that plagued Mama for several months was that her main luggage, containing most of her clothes, books, and other personal possessions, did not arrive. She had some spasmodic reports from the Peace Corps about the luggage having been sighted at various places, but still it didn't come. Rosalynn and my sisters, Gloria and Ruth, sent her some dresses based on her former size, which she had to "take up" to fit. After two months, Mama made this diary entry: "I wrote the PC again in Delhi about my bag. Guess I'll never hear. I believe the PC is the most negligent part of the U.S. gov't. I have never felt that we get a good deal."

At first, her Vikhroli supervisors provided some linen, clothing, and so on, but after a few weeks, Mama wrote, "Their anxiety to make things nice has vanished. Now I'm just another work horse." The luggage finally arrived late in March. She wrote, "Oh boy, what fun — cigarettes, toilet paper, Kleenex, my dresses — everything!" She was especially ecstatic to see the smiling face of "my darling Mickey Spillane" on some of his detective novels.

An even worse problem for Mama was the obvious distress of some couples when they were forced to accept the birth control restraints and often blamed their plight on Mama, the one delivering the bad news. Their ancient culture was based on the premise that children are the only source of support for parents in their later years — insurance against future economic disaster. Mother's diary shows that she helped with an average of four or five vasectomies each day on men she had convinced to accept sterilization. She seemed to feel guilty about each one. She wrote: "I dislike talking about vasectomies to men and cannot do it without a feeling of guilt. They resent it, and so do I. What must I do?"

Mama had a few mishaps, embarrassing to her. On her first Christmas Day in India, after they learned that both my father and I had been Lions in Plains, she was invited to attend a dedication by Lions Clubs of a community house. She was carried the last few hundred yards on a bullock cart, and when she backed away to take a photograph of the cart and driver, she stepped in a hole and badly sprained her left foot and ankle. Mama attempted to conceal her injury, which might emphasize her age, but the bruise and swelling became so great that she had to be carried back to her room in a chair. She was proud, though, that she didn't miss any workdays.

A more serious problem soon developed that hindered Mother's proper performance among the families and at the Community Center. It was extremely difficult for her to explain the sensitive and emotional issues of birth control — a subject considered taboo even among the native families — especially when the family had reached the limit of children and the only viable option was for the husband to have a vasectomy. Most of the families spoke Hindi, and Mama wrote, "Our Marathi isn't worth a damn." Her supervisor, a woman named Aloo Mowdawalla, ordained that she begin taking private lessons in Hindi.

Mama had a number of diary entries concerning talking to Aloo about the lack of progress with her language studies, and she requested a teacher who would come

111

regularly and could speak a little English. One finally came, and Mama described the first encounter: "After working until 5:30 I finally got home and found an instructor waiting for me. He taught me some sentences and then just wanted to talk about me. He asked why I came here and if I had to do this for a living — and if I have four children why can't they support me in my old age. I stood him on his ear as I described myself and greatly exaggerated my financial and social life at home. Some of the Indians have no tact. They ask, 'How old are you? Why do you have so many scratches on your face [meaning wrinkles]?'"

Mama seems to have been an attractive guest — something of a curiosity — among the rich friends of the Godrej family, and she was invited to some of the social affairs in Vikhroli, especially when foreign visitors were being entertained. Most of them spoke fluent English, and they seemed to enjoy her comments about America and the evolving political process in our country. She managed to avoid most of the affairs with the excuse of her work or not feeling well but accepted those invitations that would give her an insight into India's cultural life.

One event was a wedding reception for children of two wealthy farmers in the area.

Mama described it as "the most glamorous sight I've ever seen. At least a thousand blue, green, and yellow lights could be seen from miles away, and the guests entered on a beautiful red carpet at least a hundred yards long. Everyone was bowing to the parents, but when they saw me they came down from the dais to shake hands and make me feel at home. A great orchestra was playing Indian music, but at a sign from the bride's sister they broke into a wild American piece and the young people began dancing like my grandchildren — the frug and chicken, etc. It was a wonderful experience, and people said it cost over 50,000 rupees."

Mother was able to participate a few days later in greeting the ambassador from Iran, who visited Godrej Industries. She wrote that everyone salaamed to Mr. Godrej and the ambassador except her. She just extended her hand and said, "How do you do?"

As in Plains when she had not been on duty as a nurse, Mama dressed as simply as possible, usually in loose-fitting smocks. She wrote that she always cut her own hair, forming a knot every now and then and "cutting off all the bunches that I could see sticking out." Later, she asked a male nurse to do the same in the back. One problem was somewhat serious: she couldn't wear the only footwear available, called chappals. She had to walk about four miles each day, and the sandals formed blisters on her toes and feet that turned to sores. She began to go barefoot most of the time, as did many of the Indians with whom she was working, but caught a bus or hitched a ride on occasion. She described one trip with "eleven in the car — all adults."

She got hungry when she was too busy to shop for food or failed to get a ride into town. "Sometimes I feel like a hungry beggar who's too proud to beg and won't steal." Mama wrote us that she was losing a lot of weight, and we sent her cheese, peanut butter, and other things that could survive in the mail. We learned later that she gave most of it away.

One of the brightest spots in Mama's memories about the Peace Corps was Mr. Vinod, the gardener. Often surreptitiously, he would bring her flowers and vegetables, even cutting one of his prized rarely blooming flowers for her. She tried to pay him, but he refused, explaining that his gifts didn't really belong to him but were the property of the entire village — which meant the Godrej family. Mr. Vinod had a daughter named Madhavi, about seven years old, and in order to repay the gardener, Mama offered to

Lillian with the gardener Mr. Vinod's daughter, 1967

teach her to read and write, in English. They would go to a quiet place on the nearby hill, and one day Mr. Vinod asked permission to take their photograph together. It was later used on the cover of an edition of Mama's letters.

One of Mama's early letters indicated what a sacrifice she was making. "When I get home, I want a T-bone steak, tossed salad, a biscuit, a good drink, a haircut, a manicure, some clothes that fit, some grits, peach ice cream, a drink, some butter beans, some flowers, and a drink, the children to spend the night, the attic fan turned on, to go fishing, some collards and corn bread, my own bed, a car to ride in, my rings, a bathing suit, a good hot soaking bath to get this grime off, a drink, and some NEW American magazines! I'm trying to imagine that all will be available some day, and I intend to have it all — one thing at a time . . . as I'm sure ONE drink will knock me completely out."

Over the months, Mother's Hindi improved a little as various teachers were assigned to assist her. None of them were professional instructors or could speak English, and she and Aloo soon decided that significant further progress was unlikely. Then Mama had an idea that would let her continue her assigned work on family planning. She wrote a play about the important aspects of the family planning program — an explicit and heated discussion between a husband and wife. Then she was able to memorize a few Hindi words at a time and say them over and over until her South Georgia drawl was comprehensible. Phrase by phrase, she recorded them on a tape machine until the entire dialogue was complete. Her next step was to get one of the many local artisans to help her contrive two puppets.

In a portable theater made of sticks and burlap bags, Mama would get under the little stage and manipulate the puppets while the tape played. Although Aloo helped at first to provide an audience, groups were soon attracted to the drama, which was filled with a kind of frank sexual language that was rare among the families. These efforts began to have success, as indicated by one diary entry: "This afternoon I helped the surgeon perform thirty-three vasectomies!"

9
SEEKING A ROLE IN INDIA

During these first months in Vikhroli, my mother was known as Lilly and was respected for her skills as a registered nurse and somewhat resented because of her aversion to the strict family planning regimen that she was responsible for helping to enforce.

Aloo Mowdawalla was, in effect, Mother's boss, responsible for assigning her duties and teaching her proper courtesies and proprieties, but not always with total success. On one occasion there was a Game Day — something of a small festival — within the larger community where the workers lived, over which Mrs. Godrej presided. Mama was instructed to attend, but after an hour or so she saw that she had no role to play and left to return to her regular duties. She wrote, "When I got back to my apartment in the late afternoon, Aloo came and gave me a severe 'talking-to' about leaving while Mrs. Godrej was still there. It impressed me very little."

In Mama's diary, there was also this surprising entry: "A very bad day for me. I met with my first rudeness. I stopped a group of children from beating a small dog and got in a mess. Later they swarmed after me and were angry, I guess. Anyway, when I walked away I was hit in the back with a stone. I went back and a girl was holding a slingshot. (I also broke my dark glasses.)

"My Hindi teacher finally came after missing several days. I told him about the rock. Tears came into his eyes, and he said 'Forgive their ignorance.'"

Perhaps the teacher informed Aloo about the incident, because the next day she reached out to Mother by informing her that she could study just Marathi instead of Hindi. Despite her previous complaints, Mama realized how much she had learned and decided to stick to some knowledge of both dialects.

After her normal working hours, Mama was also permitted to moonlight as a volunteer nurse in the general clinic, under the supervision of Dr. Ghanshyam Bhatia. Mama made it obvious to everyone that her first love was working in the clinic, where she could utilize more of her medical training, and she began to write to us about her hopes that Mrs. Godrej might authorize her to help in the clinic on a more regular basis. Mama offered to forgo her annual Peace Corps vacation so she could help the overloaded doctor. After consulting with Dr. Bhatia, Mrs. Godrej approved Mama's offer.

Mother's diary entry recounted: "When I told Dr. B. I would be here and could help him several times a week he 'ecstatically' said, 'You can come.'" Later she commented, "Dr. Bhatia makes me nervous when he comes out to help me inject (when I have a rush). But he has a right to do anything he wishes. He sits all day and examines the poor people with no break."

The doctor had a small space in the corner of the clinic where he saw patients with some degree of privacy, provided by file cabinets pushed together. When Mama began giving injections and simple treatment, she noticed that two of the cabinets were separated by about six inches, so that he could watch her work. She was very excited when she recorded after a few days that the cabinets were touching each other once again.

For several weeks, Mama described her greatest ordeal in letters to us:

"It was during the drought, the weeds were up real high from the monsoon — dry, and rattling in the wind, always a hot wind blew.

I went to work one morning, and by the side of the road I heard something. I looked over, and it was a woman. And she was covered with vermin. You know what vermin are? She had both arms up, and those arms were filthy and bleeding, you know, and she was trying to crawl across the road to an embankment, where there was a trickle of water. I ran back home and got a bottle of water and a loaf of bread and tried to find someone to help me. They just laughed at me. You know, if you know Indians, they have the most terrible laughter." Later, she could imitate it, high, cold, and scornful. "I went to the doctor's office — one of our first direct talks — and he said, 'Miz Lilly, don't try to change us in the short time you'll be here. Whatever you do, don't feed her. The sooner she starves to death, the better off she'll be. She has infectious leprosy and must not be touched.'"

Mama had been in Vikhroli about six months, and she became so discouraged with language, vasectomies, not using her nursing skills, and the sight of the leprous woman, that she decided to resign from the Peace Corps and return to Plains. "India was killing me," she wrote. "I couldn't bear it any longer — the dirt, the squalor, the poverty,

121

the apparent insensitivity to the suffering of others, the restraints on my own activities. I had thought I could go and share some of my income, which is pretty good, and feed the hungry and clothe the naked and all, and I found I couldn't. I just didn't have the strength to bear the horrible cruelty and indifference.

"I went up on a little hillside, behind some rocks where I have been able to read books in solitude, and reminded God that He had sent me here to carry out some of my duties as a Christian. I just told God, 'You got me over here and unless you'll help me I'll have to go back.' While I was at it, I also prayed to God to let me have more work in the doctor's office. All right, the next morning, this little black boy stuck a note through my peephole from the doctor, saying 'Come and help me.' And that is the biggest miracle that ever happened to me."

The workload at the clinic was prodigious. Mama recorded that during one day she counted 360 patients who were diagnosed and treated, in addition to the routine injections that she gave to groups of schoolchildren. It was not unusual to administer more than 300 inoculations at a time, and one day she really enjoyed helping to give triple injections to 352 schoolchildren, but she deplored the next day's work, when she had to lecture to ten men about having vasectomies.

The end of May 1967 brought a series of anguished letters: "Food isn't good anymore. The woman is always on my mind. I'll be so glad when she's dead and moved — Oh, dear — I wonder if they will move her! The most enlightened person I know is Dr. Bhatia, who told me, 'It's the survival of the fittest, Missy. You are banging your head on a stone wall.'"

The next day, everything changed: "Oh, everything is rosy and I feel so good: The woman finally died, and they did move her, so I won't have to walk by her anymore. — My sweet little cross-eyed boy came to the Clinic for shots. He never cries, and was so happy when I gave him an old Christmas card."

She also reported her earliest experiences with treating leprosy. The first case was a small girl, about eight years old, whose parents seemed to indicate that they did not really desire to see their daughter treated. The child was very timid, perhaps about her disfigurement, and Mama dutifully notified Dr. Bhatia of her presence. The doctor replied, "Well, treat her." Mother was taken aback and requested that she be permitted to treat the other waiting patients. Brusquely, the doctor instructed her to do her duty as directed. After cleaning the sores and administering the required medicine, Mama left the clinic and walked to her apartment. There, she said, "I scrubbed myself all over until my skin was raw."

She went on to record the subsequent events, which I described later in one of my poems:

When I nursed in a clinic near Bombay,
A small girl, shielding all her leprous
    sores,
Crept inside the door. I moved away,
But then the doctor said, "You take this
    case!"
First I found a mask and put it on,
Quickly gave the child a shot and then,
Not well, I slipped away to be alone
And scrubbed my entire body red and
    raw.
I faced her treatment every week with
    dread
And loathing — for the chore, not the
    child.
As time passed, I was less afraid,
And managed not to turn my face away.
Her spirit bloomed as sores began to
    fade.

She'd raise her anxious, searching eyes to
  mine,
To show she trusted me. We'd smile and
  say
A few Marathi words, then reach and hold
Each other's hands. And then love grew
  between
Us, so that when I kissed her lips
I didn't feel unclean.

In some ways, Mama was looked upon as an untouchable because she was involved in the handling of human wastes and performed many of the personal duties that servants provided for higher-caste Indians. The caste system always bothered her, and she expressed some resentment toward Prime Minister Indira Gandhi because of this and the rigid family planning restraints that she imposed. Mama commented often about her difficulty in determining which person was supposed to perform which task — much worse than the divisions of responsibility within American labor unions.

An executive in the local bank was of special interest, as Mother observed him several times. She wrote, "The cashier has a servant to pick up the phone and hand it to him when it rings. Then when he finishes the conversation he nods slightly and the servant rushes back to replace the receiver. Now, the phone is within two feet of the cashier! When I tell them I wash my dishes & clothes and do my own cooking, they don't believe me. I wipe off the injection table and chairs at the Clinic, and clean up blood from the floor. Anyone else would lose face by doing that. I love to shock them, and they bring their friends to watch me wash off a cabinet! When I bandage a foot or leg, my patient often bends down, puts a hand on each of my feet, and salaams."

One of Mama's most interesting experiences was having tea with a middle-aged Hindu couple. "The husband and I sat on something like little pots and watched while the wife made tea. She squatted on the floor, where she had a towel which she picked up with her toes, then she pitched it in the air and caught it to wipe cups and saucers, floor, and vessel. I watched with awe, getting more unhungry by the minute. The table was about six inches high, made of cow dung, and the floors were paved with same.

"When she fixed our tea, she didn't have any for herself, and I refused to eat without her — so for the FIRST TIME, she ate with her husband. When I left, they promised me that from now on they would eat together, UNLESS someone else was there!"

Inevitably, Mama became involved in family affairs. She described one episode with a husband who took a second wife, with permission of the first, who had failed to bear a son. The second had a girl, and the husband returned to the first one, whom he seemed to prefer. Then the second wife had a son, and she came to Mama and asked her to intercede to get her husband back. Mama declined but added, "I just advised her to insert a loop in case he returns, and I gave her a rupee for the little boy."

As Mother visited the homes and some of the textile factories, she noticed that all the women sewed without thimbles. Often, their fingertips would be either sore or bleeding. Mother decided to surprise them and asked us to send her two dozen thimbles. When they arrived, she distributed them to the women and showed them how they should be used. She told us later that she saw all the thimbles being used as ornaments, mostly in the women's hair.

After I had lost my campaign for governor, Vice President Hubert Humphrey came down to Atlanta to visit in the home of his friend Marvin Shoob, one of my political supporters. I was just a farmer and former state senator, and being invited there to meet the Vice President of the United States was a great honor for me. Humphrey seemed quite weary after a long and tedious tour of Europe, but he answered the eager questions of those Georgia friends until quite late, about two o'clock in the morning.

He was well briefed, probably by the Shoobs, because when I entered the room, he said, "Young man, I met your mother one time during the last campaign, and understand that she is now in the Peace Corps in India."

I stammered, "Yes, sir, that's right."

He said, "Well, I've been very interested in the Peace Corps. The idea originally came from me, and I've been proud to see it put into effect." He added, "Where's your mother's assignment?"

"She's near Bombay."

"How's she getting along?"

"Well, she's quite lonely, sir. She's been there for quite a while, and she's not had a visit from anybody, even the Peace Corps officials. She's in a little village called Vikhroli." I noticed that one of his aides scribbled some notes.

About a month later, I got a letter from my mother telling me that the head of the Peace Corps in India had driven to Vikhroli to see her and asked if she needed anything. She said no, that she was getting along quite well, but when he insisted, she said that a ride down to Bombay would be nice. He said, "Well, can I take you shopping, Mrs. Carter?" She said, "Yes, I'd like that." So they went shopping, he bought her a very fine supper, and then he brought her back to her apartment. When he got out, he handed her a bottle of the excellent bourbon that she liked. He started to get back in the car to leave and then returned to her and said, "By the way, Miss Lillian, who in hell are you, anyway?" It was not until later that my mother knew who she was. She was a friend, once removed, of Vice President Humphrey, who had sent the Peace Corps director his instructions.

10
LEARNING THE STRANGE CUSTOMS

Mama seemed quite happy as she described how, as a nurse, she won over the small children of factory workers. "As soon as the children were brought into the clinic they began to cry. I always had some hard candy balls in my pocket, and I'd stick one in their mouths. The next day their mothers would tell me that the children wanted to come back. So they came by in droves even though they were supposed to go to another clinic."

In one instance Mama's success in convincing a reluctant patient to let her give him an insulin injection created a reputation for her. The key to her success was simple: she obtained a needle smaller than those used routinely in the clinic. "I showed the man the regular needle and my small needle and this persuaded him. He told everybody that I was an expert, and soon I had my group of loyal patients. The doctor said, 'What did you do to that man?' and I said, 'Oh I don't know; it's probably my charm.'"

During these first months in the clinic, the doctor treated Mama almost as a subservient untouchable, but she seemed to revere him. She commented to us on his critical remarks about America: "I helped Doctor Bhatia in the clinic all a.m. He is always on the offensive about Americans, saying that we who leave our country to go elsewhere must be cowards. Despite this, I think he's wonderful and I told him how much good he could do to go to America and lecture on things he does. He actually sees more different kinds of diseases each month than some of our doctors do in a lifetime."

After a few months of working in the clinic, Mama began describing to us her frustration at being forbidden to treat anyone except the five thousand factory workers and their families who lived in the village:

"People from the hills stop me on my way to work and beg me to do something for them. I try to carry a little first aid bag, and I do whatever I can, right there in the middle of the road. A few days ago I was sitting by the window in the office when a woman knocked on the bars — we have bars and shutters for windows — and asked me to feel her breast. By the way, I used a little of the Hindi language, since she didn't speak

Marathi. Anyway, her breast was hard as a rock. I stole some belladonna plaster that I had seen the doctor use for infection and I told her how to put it on. I gave her a handful of painkillers that I also stole from the clinic. In about two weeks her breast was down; it was healed."

A few weeks later, she wrote, "I became increasingly frustrated about those who were obviously ill but were excluded from any health services, but Dr. Bhatia was not about to bend the rules. I finally couldn't stand it any more, and I decided to go to one of the Godrej brothers who owned the complex. He was a man so rich, you don't go to him; he had to send for you. And when he would come into the clinic, the doctor would bow almost down to his ankles. I had gotten to know this man socially and I decided to go to his office.

"When I walked in, I started crying, and he said, 'Lilly, what's the matter?'

"When I told him, he said, 'No one is rich enough to help all those people.'

"I said, 'Then I'll have to go home. I cannot stand this any longer.' And I even added, falsely, 'Jimmy's writing to me to come home.'

"Finally he told me that if I could get the doctor to see more people, and if we could get medicine, and if I would stand by the gate and only let people through who I felt were sick enough, he would permit it.

"It was against the Peace Corps rules, but I cashed a personal check for a hundred dollars' worth of rupees. I put the money in a box and took it in to Dr. Bhatia. When I told him whom I'd seen, he almost fainted. He kind of blew his stack when he heard about it, but he finally took the money to buy drugs.

"I also did something else. On Monday mornings, we would have two drug salesmen come in, one from Parke-Davis and the other from Eli Lilly. The first one I met was the Parke-Davis man. I told him if he would give me some samples I would write to Mr. Parke and Mr. Davis — 'whom I know personally' — and tell them the good work he was doing. He emptied his bag and gave me all the samples he had.

"But when I saw the Eli Lilly man, I was in a mess. I couldn't remember whether Eli Lilly was dead or alive. So I did the same thing, only I said, 'My son went to school with his grandson or grandnephew, I don't remember which.' I soon had two cabinets full of medicine."

Having no money, Mama also urged me and others to contact pharmaceutical companies to send her free samples and "surplus" medicines. She soon created a well-stocked American-style free clinic, or at least a more adequate first aid station.

One of the high points of Mama's stay at Vikhroli is best described in her own words: "Mrs. Godrej sent word for me to write a little report about any improvements needed and where I think I can fit in best. Well, I sent my notes the next day and I was called at the doctor's office letting me know that Mrs. Godrej was sending her limousine and driver to bring me to headquarters. I was scared pea-green. I just knew she was going to criticize my report as I told her everything. Well, Mr. Godrej met me at the door and took me to the office where he, Mrs. G., and an architect were looking at plans for a new hospital. They told me to look it over and, from my American standpoint, give them advice. I did. They took down everything I said, made changes accordingly, and I finally asked them to call Dr. Bhatia and they sent for him. We left two hours later, and Mr. Godrej said, 'We'll have another meeting of the staff when the architect makes all the changes.'"

Most of Mama's diary entries about home concerned our failing to write to her often enough and not sending her enough books to read, but every now and then one of her entries has reminded me of milestone family events. On March 20, 1967, she wrote: "Oh, the most wonderful news from Jimmy yesterday! They are expecting a baby in October. I couldn't be happier about an event. Just do hope that Rosalynn will take care of herself. Some days I feel like I can't take it — then something like this happens for my morale and all is right again." (Amy was born seven months later.)

As Christmas approached, we children and grandchildren consulted with one another about what to send Mama. We knew she could not receive any money other than her tiny salary from the Peace Corps, so we tried to select about a dozen small things that we thought she might be missing. She wrote an ecstatic letter of thanks, but about a week later, after gifts were exchanged on New Year's Day in India, she reluctantly reported that she had given them all away — "one by one." She asked us to remember that each of our gifts had brought two people happiness, both her and the second recipient. The most enthusiastic response was from her roommate, Mabel, who received a jar of mustard.

■ ■ ■ ■

Mama usually avoided the various assemblies of the Peace Corps, but she attended one in Goa in January 1968. She had been cold in Vikhroli, so we were pleased when she wrote that she had splurged and bought what she described as "a beautiful cashmere shawl." Not surprisingly, she wore it to the clinic on her first day back on the job and later reported that "one of the patients came in with pneumonia, and since we have no blankets, I wrapped my shawl around, and let him take it on home, I guess to keep. Material things have lost all meaning for me.

"Also, I'm not as susceptible to starvation and hungry looks as I was. I can stand it better when I realize I cannot save the world, so I must work harder and do more for the ones I contact — not in family planning but in friendship and understanding."

About a month after her first Christmas in India, Dr. Bhatia asked Mother if she would consider joining a discussion group led by his cousin. She agreed, and then discovered that she would be the only woman involved and that the usual subjects were religion and philosophy. She reported to us that "Mr. Bhatia" was the most perfect person she had ever met — "So damned good you can't imagine him going to the bathroom" was the way she expressed it.

On one occasion they asked Mama to lead the next discussion, which would be a comparison of health care and medicines in America and India. She told them that Peace Corps rules prevented her from speaking on any subject involving comparisons, because that could be construed as "political." To us, she added, "I didn't give the real reason — that I don't have enough sense!"

It was obvious that Mama was being overly modest, because she was soon participating in the discussions. She explained that she had nerve enough to do this because she realized that most of the men could rarely understand what she was saying — either in their language or when she spoke English with her Georgia accent. After a few months of these weekly discussions, Mr. Bhatia invited her to accompany him to a lecture by the great swami Chinmayananda.

An enormous crowd surrounded the revered teacher, but after his lecture and a dialogue with the audience, Mother and Mr. Bhatia's discussion group were permitted to meet him personally. He chatted with her for a few moments, then allowed her to take a photograph. She added, "The greatest part of all, though, was the fact that he

Lillian in a session with swami and others, 1967

LOOKED at me once — this is considered the highest honor of all!" Shortly thereafter, Mr. Bhatia informed Mama that it was his intention to shake her hand on her final day in India.

The most anguished cry that came from our mother during her time in India was early in June 1968. She reported that her heart was broken and that all the efforts of her friends and co-workers were fruitless in easing her pain. Bobby Kennedy had been assassinated. This was the first time, she said, that she had completely lost control of herself.

On her seventieth birthday, just a few days before leaving India, she wrote, "I am seventy years old today, and I think of where I am, and what I'm doing, and why. When Earl died, my life lost its meaning and direction. For the first time, I lost my will to live. Since that time, I've tried to make my life have some significance. I felt useful when I was at Auburn, serving as housemother for my bad, sweet K.A.'s. And I'm glad I worked at the Nursing Home, but God forbid that I ever have to live in one!

"I didn't dream that in this remote corner of the world, so far away from the people and material things that I had always considered so necessary, I would discover what Life is really all about, sharing yourself with others — and accepting their love for you is the most precious gift of all.

"If I had one wish for my children, it would be that each of you would dare to do the things and reach for goals in your own lives that have meaning for you as individuals, doing as much as you can for everybody, but not worrying if you don't please everyone.

"When I look back over my life, I see the

pieces fit — it has been a planned life, and I truly believe God had everything to do with it."

When she left Vikhroli, heading home, several villagers walked twelve miles to the airport and stood beside Mama's plane crying. "I left part of my heart there," she said.

Mama gave away her remaining money and most of her possessions before leaving, but she had to retain the last-minute gifts that she received. With a few personal items, these filled a fairly large suitcase. She was afraid she would lose her luggage if she checked it all the way to Atlanta, and when she disembarked at London's Heathrow Airport, she discovered that she would have a long walk to her next plane. All she had was the heavy suitcase and ten cents. After she stood alone for a while, a porter noticed her and offered his assistance. She said she couldn't afford it and explained her predicament. He listened carefully and then said, "Ma'am, it would be an honor for me to help you." After delivering her to the proper gate and checking her luggage, he refused her offer of the ten-cent tip. She made him give her his name and address, and her first task when she arrived in Plains was to send him her effusive thanks and perhaps the largest tip he had ever received.

In a later news interview about the Peace Corps, Mama summarized her feelings in a few words: "In India, what I did was help people who didn't have anything. I'm not quoting the Bible because I don't know it that well, but it says that when you do something for somebody in need you get back a hundredfold. I got it back a thousandfold."

11
EXPANDING INTERESTS

As a surprise homecoming gift for Mama, we decided to rebuild the burned Pond House on the same site overlooking her favorite fishing lake. It was a more modern two-story house with the main room mostly enclosed by a large fireplace on one end and nothing else except picture windows — with no curtains. Mama was delighted with the gift, and over the years she increasingly considered this her primary residence.

We installed one of the first huge satellite dishes overlooking the pond, and Mama was able to monitor a wide range of televised sporting events, including Auburn's football games, professional basketball, and the major league achievements of her beloved Dodgers. She also tried to watch every tennis match in which Jimmy Connors played.

Mama began accepting a few invitations as a public speaker, and she was soon making one or two speeches every week. She never asked for a fee but insisted on transportation and lodging at her destination. She recorded a total of 670 public appearances, with general themes of service in the Peace Corps or not letting age or timidity be a barrier to a full and adventurous life. She never prepared a text and had only a hazy idea of what she was going to say. She would sometimes talk for an hour or more, including a general discussion with people in the audience. She never really liked to wear shoes and often got barefoot before or during her speech. Mama was completely unrestrained, and I still have members of some churches tell me of her apparently forgetting or not caring about the language she used to their staid congregations — especially when describing some of her work with family planning in India.

Before, during, and after my time in the White House, Mama became a favorite guest on the talk shows of Johnny Carson, Merv Griffin, and others, where her discussions were even more lively and irrepressible than her public speeches. I remember that, when Carson retired, there was a long retrospective show with excerpts from some of his favorite interviews. An extended segment was included of him and Mother discussing farm life in her early married years. The conversation began to focus on Mama's description of the outdoor toilet that our family used before we had water and electricity in our home. Since we had a "two-holer," one for adults and the other for us children, there was a deteriorating explanation of how one was higher, lower, above, or below the other. On what might have been considered a higher plane, she was frequently interviewed by Walter Cronkite about national politics.

Some of the high points of my mother's life were her visits to Las Vegas and Reno, where she formed friendships with Carson, Griffin, Dean Martin, Frank Sinatra, and Andy Williams. They would make arrangements for her to spend two or three days at one of the casinos where they had a financial interest or were performing. When she arrived, there would be a stylish dress or two lying across the bed in her suite, along with tickets to some of the more popular shows in town and an invitation to play blackjack. We children never understood how Mama could be so lucky, but she managed to win about fifteen hundred dollars during each visit. We presumed that, if the dealer was helping her, the casino was the voluntary loser.

I became governor soon after my mother returned from India, and I completely reorganized the state government. One major change was to bring multiple small agencies into a single Department of Human Resources, with jurisdiction over all state health and welfare programs. Based on her lifetime of service as a registered nurse, for which she still retained her license, and her special experiences in India, I appointed Mama to the board of governors of the department. The commissioner of the department was Richard Harden, and they were soon intimate friends. Richard became director of the federal Office of Administration while I was in Washington and volunteered to accompany Mother on some of the official trips that I asked her to make.

For their Christmas present one year, Billy and Sybil stocked Mama's pond with full-size rainbow trout, which all of us knew could not survive during the summer months, when water temperatures always became too high. Mama assumed the delightful task of catching all of them before it was too late. Ordinarily very generous, she prohibited anyone fishing in what always had been our family's pond unless she was in the boat and personally involved.

Mother was very careful to conceal her mistakes and injuries. She bruised easily, and when we would detect any discoloration or scraped places on her arms or legs, she would always deny knowing about them

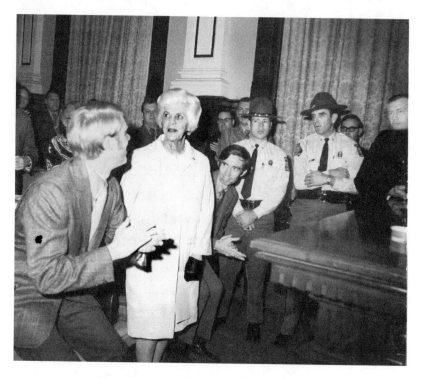
Grandson Jack and Lillian at Jimmy's
inauguration as governor, 1971

or discount their significance. I remember once when she drove from the Pond House to our farm supply office with a hook deeply embedded in her arm, with the rod, reel, and line still attached. We cut off the hook, threaded it through her flesh to accommodate the barb, applied some antiseptic and a Band-Aid, and she returned to her boat.

By this time my sister Ruth Carter Stapleton had become a noted author and had expanded her Christian ministry to a worldwide scale, and Mother and Gloria accompanied Ruth to some of the retreats. They also attended many sessions of Camps Farthest Out, which Ruth would lead. Both Ruth and Mother strove to find the most practical possible ways of applying their religious faith to everyday life. Participants have sent me some recordings of Mama's impromptu talks. She was able to intertwine her own experiences with whatever biblical passage was being discussed.

I always felt during those years when Mama, Billy, Sybil, Gloria, Rosalynn, and I all lived in Plains that Mama and Billy were especially close, perhaps because they shared such an intense interest in sports. Billy had an encyclopedic knowledge of baseball, and he and Mama had detailed discussions of the teams, players, and their statistics that were far beyond what the rest of us could understand.

In fact, Billy and Sybil had their first date in 1951 as young teenagers when Mama and Daddy took them to a Class D baseball game in nearby Americus. They never dated anyone else, and Sybil still remembers the advice she received from Mama before their marriage a few years later: "First, I have some strong-willed children. Don't ever back down or give in to them, and don't go to bed without resolving your differences." She paused a few seconds and then added, "Also, don't ever bring me a half a cup of cold coffee. It has to be full, hot, and black."

Later, during the summer of 1976, Billy and I were the captains of opposing softball teams, both of us pitchers. I was the Democratic nominee for president, and Plains was flooded with curious tourists, almost all of them attending our daily contests. There were days when we had several thousand people surrounding the field in front of the schoolhouse. The Atlanta Braves had a miserable team that year, and there were often more fans in Plains than in Atlanta. One of the best days that Mama and Billy (and I) ever shared was when we hosted the entire Braves team, led by its owner, Ted Turner, and the baseball icon Hank Aaron, for a visit to Plains.

Mama lived alone in her house in town, and she liked to take in boarders — without charge, but they could pay for some groceries on occasion. She ran something like a free bed-and-breakfast. There were always federal agricultural inspectors stationed in Plains to determine the value of each load of peanuts that farmers brought to our warehouse for sale or storage. Mama would usually invite one of them to stay with her. Once, when we were able to recruit a young doctor to establish his practice in our town, he and his wife moved in with her and stayed until they could find a permanent home. During school vacation times, one of the grandchildren would spend the entire period there, and when Rosalynn and I were seeking votes during the early days of my campaigns, Amy lived with Mama. Mother also more or less adopted two special friends, James Day, a construction worker, and Randy Coleman, who sometimes helped Billy at the warehouse. They lived with her when their work brought them to the community. Mama liked company if she could select each person carefully, but she still had certain rules.

One of Mama's most memorable experiences with a lodger occurred when Randy and Billy killed a large rattlesnake and decided to cook and serve it as the main course at a supper for their friends. Randy cleaned the serpent, wrapped it carefully, and put it in Mama's refrigerator. Later, when she was preparing to cook supper, she unwrapped the snake. She screamed at the top of her lungs, threw the snake across the room, found Randy, cursed him out, and made him take every item out of the refrigerator and freezer, throw the food away, and scour all the wire shelves and walls with soap and then baking soda.

My mother loved soap operas, especially *All My Children.* We knew not to visit or call her when it was on, because she wouldn't open the door or answer the telephone. In September 1976, Ruth Warrick learned of Mama's addiction to the program and paid a visit to Plains. After returning to Hollywood, Miss Warrick informed the *Los Angeles Times:*

"I'd heard that Miss Lillian drops everything and dismisses everyone from her presence at 12:15 p.m. every weekday to watch 'All My Children,' and I got it in my head that I wanted to interview her for an autobiographical memoir I'm writing called 'Phoebe Tyler, Phoebe Tyler.' So I simply called her.

"'You're coming to see me, Mrs. Tyler?' Miss Lillian exclaimed. 'Well, I couldn't be more pleased.' Then she said, 'Why, you must stay over 'til Sunday mornin' to meet my son and attend church services with us.' I allowed as how I could do that.

"It was the most fantastic two days of my life. Saturday afternoon I chatted with Miss Lillian about her years as a Peace Corps volunteer in India. Would you believe she was 70 years old? And she advised me what Phoebe should do in the 'All My Children' story line: 'You should get rid of that stick-in-the-mud husband of yours,' she insisted. 'You've got a lot of spunk in you, but you should get out and maybe get another man. The Shah of Iran would be just perfect.'

"We both agreed that Phoebe would be happier if she devoted her time to service to humanity rather than scheming to break up other people's happiness. After all, concern for your fellow man is the greatest reward.

"After our talk Miss Lillian arranged a tour of the town, and I was treated like Queen Elizabeth. Everyone I met said as how I didn't seem at all like Phoebe. They forced me to talk like Phoebe in that haughty, imperious tone of voice, which they loved. That night at a party for his campaign workers, the Peanut Brigade, Mr. Carter walked right over and kissed me. My dear, I almost fainted.

"But the most incredible experience was attending church with the Carters. I sat between Amy and Miss Lillian, who said, 'Now honey, sitting in our family pew is an experience nobody's ever had before.'

"It was like going back to my youth. Not many people know I was raised as a Southern Baptist back in St. Joe, Missouri. In fact, I once preached a sermon in Kansas City. You see, at eighteen I came off the mountain and wanted to be a missionary. Anyway, hearing Jimmy talk to the congregation about being reborn rekindled the spiritual flame in me. I haven't been exactly wicked in my life, but I haven't been an angel either. There must be something more than hollow fame. I'm at a crossroads myself.

"I can't tell you what meeting the Carters has done for me. I'm still floating. The South has risen again and so has Ruth Warrick.

"Miss Lillian's parting advice to me was, 'You be sweet, you hear!' "

A month later, when campaigning throughout New England, Mama was escorted to a rally of senior citizens in New York. The first to greet her was Ruth Warrick, who presented to her a hand-painted poster containing the photographs and autographs of all the actors in *All My Children*. Mama announced to the crowd, "I won't talk to anyone when that show is on, and I'd like to introduce you to the star — the meanest woman in the world."

"I play Phoebe Tyler, the woman you love to hate," Miss Warrick said. The audience responded, "Yeah, yeah," indicating that they were also addicted to the show.

All of her grandchildren liked to stay with Mama, because she usually permitted them to do whatever they wished. They could stay up late, watch television or play games, or drive to Americus for hamburgers and a movie. She also liked to teach them, in her own way, to think for themselves and to be original.

A favorite pastime was to put the younger grandchildren on the stairs to the second floor, with a clear view through the front door, solid at bottom and transparent at top — something like a TV or movie screen. A steady stream of people would go by on the sidewalk or street, and Mama would pick out one every now and then and tell a story (real or imagined) about the person. Then she would make the children do the same, each striving to demonstrate the wildest imagination but to include a moderate degree of logic. Possibly as a result of this pastime, four of Sybil's children became either authors or playwrights.

Mama's chances to attend professional baseball or basketball games were rare, but wrestling was available just an hour's drive from her home each Wednesday night in

Columbus, Georgia. She was there every week, usually escorted by a local farmer, Troy Hunt. Mama had a raucous voice and was soon known — and loved — by all the wrestlers and the impresarios who orchestrated the events.

Her favorite was Mr. Wrestling II, who was always masked and whose real name was Johnny "Rubberman" Walker. He was what is known as a "face" wrestler — always a hero to the fans, and one of the first "good guys" to wear a mask. His primary opponents were known as The Assassin, The Spoiler, the Minnesota Wrecking Crew, etc. When I began my campaign for governor of Georgia, Mama suggested that I go with her to a match, to be introduced to the crowd. Somewhat reluctantly, I climbed into the ring during the opening ceremonies, and the announcer began to introduce me as a political candidate. There was an overwhelming chorus of boos and catcalls from the fans, who resented politics being injected into the purity of their chosen sport. When the derision subsided, the announcer said, "He's Miss Lillian's son," and all the boos turned to applause and approbation.

After the matches that night, I was honored by a chance to meet Mr. Wrestling II, and Mama suggested that we have a photograph made of my subduing the wrestler with a headlock. The photo was used during my successful campaign and is still displayed prominently in one of the historical exhibits on Main Street in Plains.★

When I had served as governor for almost two years, I decided to run for president and came from Atlanta to our home in Plains one weekend to tell Mother about my plans. After getting settled in our own house, I went to some nearby tennis courts and played a few sets. Then I walked over to Mama's house, somewhat nervous, and propped my feet on the corner of her coffee table. She said, with no respect for a governor, "Get your dirty feet off of my table!" After some preliminary discussion, I told her that I had made a very important decision and wanted her to know it.

"Well, what is it, Jimmy?"

"Mama, I've decided to run for president."

★ Almost twenty-five years later, a couple of schoolteachers bought the building lot adjacent to our home in Plains and soon erected a house of their own. Rosalynn and I went over to greet them shortly after they moved in and learned, to our delight, that it was Mr. Wrestling II and his wife, Andrea.

Startled, she asked, "President of *what?*"

After I responded, she first thought I was teasing, but after I answered her detailed questions for almost an hour, she finally said, "I think you can do it, and I want to help."

When asked later in a news interview what her first thoughts were on hearing my plan to run, she replied, "Well I was pleased. I figured that if he was elected president, someone would open a good restaurant in Plains."

12
HELPING A SON
BECOME PRESIDENT

When the time came for my active campaign to begin, after I left the governor's office early in 1975, Rosalynn and I decided that the best contribution Mama could make was to keep our eight-year-old daughter, Amy, almost on a full-time basis. Mama readily agreed, but after a few months she began insisting that she join the others in our family on the campaign trail as she had done during the governor's election of 1970. Rosalynn's mother, Allie, also lived in Plains and was eager to share the responsibility for Amy.

After analyzing the domestic and international issues and devising our overall strategy for the nationwide effort, we evolved a relatively unpublicized technique for winning the election. We decided that each of us family members would be on the road five days a week, with seven simultaneous campaigns. Rosalynn and I always went to separate states, as did our three sons, Jack, Chip, and Jeff (with their wives). Later in the campaign, Mother and her younger sister Emily (Sissy) joined us, while Rosalynn's mother kept Amy. We returned each weekend to our home in Plains, where we shared our experiences, made sure that we were all "preaching the same sermon," attended church services, drove to Atlanta for a political rally, and then went back out for another five days. All of this was, of course, coordinated by our campaign committee, headed by Hamilton Jordan. My brother, Billy, and his wife, Sybil, plus two partners, ran our Carter's Warehouse business.

I worked on the campaign full-time for eighteen months, in all fifty states, and Rosalynn concentrated on the most crucial contests, including spending seventy-five days in Florida and visiting 105 different towns in Iowa. Mama's diary showed that she met with more than five hundred groups of potential supporters, making about five stops a day. We had practically no money, and all of us resolved never to spend the night in a hotel or motel if we could find some local family to take us in. By the time the other candidates realized what was going on, we had won the Democratic primary contests in Iowa, New

Hampshire, and Florida — and then it was too late to stop us.

During the springtime months of 1976, Plains was flooded with news reporters from around the world, and all the members of our family had interminable requests for interviews. Since Mama lived in the town and frequently helped in our national campaign headquarters in the local train depot, she was especially afflicted. There were some false or distorted newspaper reports about her that she resented. A *Washington Post* cartoon showed her leaving an outdoor privy with straw coming out of her ears. One article said that she personally disliked Alabama's governor, George Wallace, and another compared her unfavorably with the Kennedys, claiming that she wore cheap drip-dry dresses. She commented to one reporter, "I'm not rich — don't put that in the paper — but I'm not poor either. I always drive a Cadillac and I just paid three hundred dollars for a dress. I think that's enough, don't you?" Another reporter described her as a "Rose Kennedy without hair dye."

A *Washington Post* article in July reported:

Her most striking quality is her stubborn, unfettered openness — a gritty take-it-or-

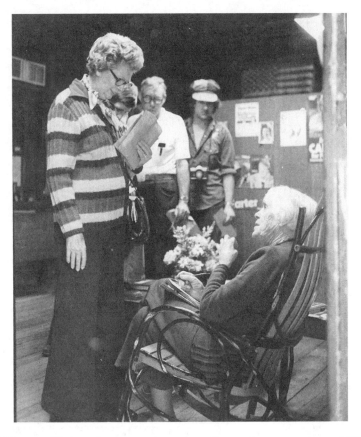

Lillian at Plains depot, welcoming Jimmy's supporters, 1976

leave-it bluntness that fits into the white-gloved orthodoxy of political motherhood as incongruously as a peanut farmer in the White House. . . . For instance, while the son promises never to tell a lie, his mother readily confesses to fibbing now and then. "I have to make up for Jimmy," she explains. She told another reporter, "I lie all the time. I have to — to balance the family ticket."

Art Buchwald's column of July 22, 1976, in a mock exchange, began with the Republicans' query, "I think we can handle Carter and Mondale, but what are we going to do about the kid and the mother?" According to Buchwald, the Republicans explored condemning Amy for doubling her lemonade price to ten cents but decided that they couldn't knock the free enterprise system. One skeleton in her closet, he wrote, was found to be "saved from a Halloween party." When they turned to my seventy-seven-year-old mother, the decision was made that she looked like everyone would want their own mothers to look, and that her demonstrated prowess on talk shows was formidable enough in itself to win the election. They were also afraid to alienate her friends like Walter Cronkite. Their only alternative was to find their own Amy and Miss Lillian, but they finally realized it was a hopeless cause.

With tongue in cheek, the news media did attempt to make a case out of Amy's lemonade prices being raised from five cents to ten cents. To quote a June 1976 article in *The New York Times:*

But Mr. Carter, the Democratic presidential hopeful, said he thought the price hike was justified. "The girls have made sub-

161

Lillian, San Donaldson, and other reporters, 1976

stantial capital improvements," the candidate observed, pointing out that they had switched from a cardboard stand to a wooden one and had swept the leaves from the area. Mr. Carter was not sympathetic to reporters who suggested a special discount for the working press. "Reporters should pay double," Mr. Carter said with a grin, "because they are on expense accounts."

One of the uncomfortable developments in Plains as I gained political strength was that various interest groups descended on our town to gain publicity for their causes. They knew the international news media would be present wherever I showed up, and the only certain place to encounter my family was each Sunday morning at Plains Baptist Church. There would be several thousand people jammed into the churchyard, with placards, banners, T-shirts, and other advertisements, pushing and shoving to gain a prominent site in view of the television cameras. They also jammed the sanctuary early in the morning, and finally we deacons had to keep the church doors locked so that our 150 or so regular worshipers could attend the sermon after they completed Sunday School in a different part of the church.

Our family members all agreed that we should try to penetrate the crowds without responding to their importunities or to the questions of the horde of news reporters. Despite this, in July 1976 Helen Dewar reported in *The Washington Post:*

A short, compact, vigorous woman whose tanned, deeply lined face is framed by a cap of white hair, Miss Lillian is always in motion and usually talking. She can say outrageous things and her soft, South Georgia drawl makes them sound more genteel than they sometimes are. As "Miss Lillian" Carter arrived for church services

Sunday, a British television correspondent thrust a microphone in her face and asked if she could explain why some people don't understand her son. "Some people," she drawled sweetly, "are just dumb."

Mother finally moved out of Plains to her more private Pond House and declared that she would grant no further interviews. One day, Press Secretary Jody Powell called her and requested just one more, very special because the reporter represented *The Washington Post*.

Mama hesitated and then asked, "Man or woman?"

Jody replied, "It's a woman."

Mama said, "Absolutely not!"

Jody sought my help, and we finally persuaded her to make this one important exception.

When the reporter arrived at the Pond House, Mama instructed her that she would not answer any questions about my boyhood, because all of it was covered in my book *Why Not the Best?* Soon, however, an inevitable question came:

"Miss Lillian, your son claims that he will never tell a lie. Do you believe him when he says this?"

Mama: "Well, Jimmy has always been

Mama had some pleasant interviews, including this one with Trude Feldman, 1976

truthful, and I have confidence that he won't change."

Reporter: "Do you mean that he has never in his life told a lie?"

After a short pause, Mama replied, "Well maybe a little white lie every now and then."

The reporter leaned forward with her microphone and said, "Aha! Aha! And what do you mean by a 'little white lie'?"

Mama said, "Well do you remember a few minutes ago when I met you at the door and said that you look very nice and that I was glad to see you?"

■ ■ ■ ■

Although Mama never counseled me on domestic or foreign issues except during the privacy of our time at home on Saturday afternoons, she sent me messages through the news media. One time, she said that her son should "quit that stuff about never telling a lie and being a Christian and how he loves his wife more than the day he met her. It is much more important for him to choose a 'good-looking' running mate." She was always concerned about my becoming too "bigheaded," as our successes mounted. Once, she commented to *Time* magazine that "there was really nothing outstanding about Jimmy as a boy," contending that both Gloria and Billy were actually the two smartest of her brood.

Quite early during my presidency, I learned to expect Mama's unvarnished comments. One AP story in April 1977 quoted her claiming that she always listened to Congressman Andrew Young, but not to me. First, she denied recently calling Andy a "windbag"; then she went on to say, "Well, he does talk a lot, but he's the only one I listen to. These days, Jimmy is too full of politics."

She also commented one day, under circumstances we never learned, "Sometimes, when I look at my children, I wish I had remained a virgin." This also became a question in Trivial Pursuit.

Mother tried to avoid the still-sensitive subject of race relations during my campaign and to let me handle it, but she told one reporter, "Amy attends an integrated school in Plains, which has nineteen black children and five whites in her beginning class. She loves it and doesn't know the difference between black and white. That is what I strive to teach her."

During one of my recording sessions with Mama in the spring of 1976, she asked, "Jimmy, do you think Earl knows that you might be President? I know that if my Papa knew it, he might jump right out of heaven. I think they know, but I'm not sure I'll know Earl as my husband when we're both there." I replied that Jesus seemed to agree with her, saying that a woman who had several husbands on earth wouldn't look on any of them as her husband after death. Jesus didn't comment on her situation, of having just one husband, so we decided they would know each other.

Mama had a great time during the festivities surrounding the 1976 Democratic Convention in New York. She was quoted in the *Los Angeles Times* as saying, "I have this feeling of awe. It is like a sacred thing. I've never experienced that before about Jimmy. It was like a voice from" — she gestured toward the ceiling — "you know, up there." To change the subject, she then denied that I got my big smile from her. She said it came from my father. "I used to say to my husband, 'You smile all day long, but you frown when you come home.'"

Mama complained about making almost an ultimate sacrifice during the campaign: not watching her favorite soap operas, *All My Children* and *The Young and the Restless*. She made careful arrangements for Gloria to watch the episodes and write everything down.

To give her a special task, I asked Mama to help Rosalynn identify some women who could serve in my administration. She (and I) were fascinated with Barbara Jordan, whom we happened to see one night on television. Mama said, "Listen, everyone, be quiet. This is the most remarkable speech I've ever heard. I've told Jimmy that woman is dynamite, and I have something — not vice president — in mind for her. My choice for vice president is Wendell Anderson [governor of Minnesota]. It's because he's so good-looking, and he speaks so-o-o-o beautifully."*

The New York Times reported my mother's birthday party in August 1976 as

> a strange and interesting New York phenomenon. She let everyone know that her son had called her at six a.m. the previous day to wish her a happy birthday — a day too early — but this was one time that she was inclined to excuse his error. She explained, "He got the wrong day, because everyone told him it was yesterday."
>
> The party's host didn't know half the guests, and Miss Lillian didn't know the host, or, for that matter, the other half of the guests. New Yorker Richard Weisman had asked some Democratic Party bigwigs if he could be of help, and he got Miss Lillian, a not inconsiderable coup that put him at least four rungs up in the week's status sweepstakes.

The *Times* also noted that the party guests included several ambassadors, governors, a

* Later, Barbara Jordan declined my offer of a cabinet post, and I chose another Minnesotan, Fritz Mondale, to be my running mate.

dozen Carter family members, Walter Mondale, Hubert Humphrey, and the mayoral candidate Ed Koch. Mama said that, for her, the most prominent guest was Tom Mc-Millen, the Atlanta Hawks basketball player, who served her a drink. "I thought he was standing on a chair," she said.

Mama described her New York visit as a temporary interruption in her preferred life. "I'm not a city gal," she said. "I'm a country hick. When this is all over, I'm going to watch my soap operas and sit there and fish for a solid month." Interviewed in Central Park, where she was sitting on a statue of Alice in Wonderland, Amy seemed to agree. She was asked, "What do you think of the Democratic Convention?" "Not much," she said. "I'd rather be home climbing trees."

My mother's favorite traveling companion was Richard Harden, whom she had known while working in Georgia's Department of Human Resources. Richard described a typical tour during the 1976 general election campaign. Mama was afflicted by the same confusions of any other campaigner with a rushed schedule and many appearances, and she refused to change her personal biases.

Accompanied by Richard, Mama had gone first to Connecticut and then to New York City, where she was scheduled to attend a political rally and fund-raiser. She was met at the airport by Mayor Abe Beame and a group of city officials, and they traveled downtown with a full police escort, sirens wailing. An aide in the front seat of the limousine was constantly talking on the radio while the mayor extolled the virtues of his city and explained to my mother that I had an excellent chance for a clear victory. President Gerald Ford, my opponent, was very unpopular, and a copy of the New York *Daily News* notorious front-page headline — FORD TO NEW YORK: "DROP DEAD" — was presented to Mama. After a few quiet signals from the aide, the motorcade was halted and Mayor Beame escorted my mother into a restaurant for a cup of coffee, a doughnut, and a casual conversation. The aide whispered to Richard that the expected crowd was slow in gathering and they were stalling for time.

When they finally arrived at the rally site, Mama motioned Richard aside, nodded toward the mayor, and whispered, "Richard, who is that nice little man?"

Richard added, "The rally was a big event at a senior citizens' center, and one old man presented Miss Lillian with a dozen roses and tried to kiss her. She pretended that someone called her, looked quickly around, and stuck the roses in his face. She never did like to be kissed or hugged, unless it was someone young and attractive."

My mother did not travel around the country during the last few weeks of the general election campaign. Instead, she assumed a much more difficult job at the small railroad depot in Plains, our original national campaign headquarters. Thousands of visitors flooded the town — all eager to catch a glimpse of some of our family members — and dozens of news reporters came just to talk about me to my friends and neighbors. Mama spent as much time as possible on the depot platform, trying to be nice to everyone who stood in line to speak to her. They were all warned by a large printed sign, "Don't touch Miss Lillian, just speak to her, and keep moving."

On election night, Rosalynn and I were in the huge Atlanta convention center, where I made a victory statement, and we had a brief celebration when I was elected. My mother led more unrestrained festivities in Plains, and we were able to join them the next morning, shortly before daybreak.

I spent the next few weeks preparing for my administration, and Mama loaned us the Pond House, in which vice-president-elect

Fritz Mondale and I met with busloads of experts on various issues that we would have to address in the White House. This was a good opportunity for me to size up the men and women whom I later invited to serve in my cabinet.

When it was time for us to go to Washington for the inauguration ceremony, President Gerald Ford sent the plane he used as Air Force One to pick up our family. In high spirits, we formed a motorcade in Plains and started the thirty-five-mile trip down to the Albany airport. We had been driving about fifteen minutes when we realized that Mama was missing! Everyone had thought that someone else would pick her up. We stopped immediately. I raced back to her home and found her, stony-faced and furious, sitting in her living room. Her first comment to me was, "I've decided to stay at home and not attend the inauguration."

She was soon persuaded to go with us, but she never let us forget that we had left her behind. She was the one who said, "We're late, through no fault of mine, but if the damned plane won't wait for us, then you'd just as well not be president!"

After my inaugural speech, our immediate family walked down Pennsylvania Avenue, and then we joined Mama and others in a solar-heated but frigid tent to watch the parade. When it was finally over, we moved as a group toward the White House, surrounded by news reporters who were eager to get any kind of personal quote. Press Secretary Jody Powell shouted, "Let's stay close together, and don't any of you talk to the press." Mama stopped and said, "Jody, you can go to hell. I'll talk to whom I please." She was immediately surrounded by television and radio microphones, and the first question was, "Miss Lillian, aren't you proud of your son?" I leaned forward to hear her answer: "Which one?"

During our first week in the White House, we had a reception just for the families who had been our hosts for a night during the campaign. There were more than seven hundred of them, and Mama stood in the receiving line with us and handed out to each one a small brass plaque that said, A MEMBER OF THE CARTER FAMILY SLEPT HERE.

13
A HELPFUL BODYGUARD

The other children and I faced a quandary concerning my seventy-eight-year-old mother when I became president, in that it was obvious she would be very active but had no staff or security. In addition to her visits to the White House and later overseas missions representing the federal government and campaigning for Democratic candidates, she continued to ride the Trailways bus to Atlanta every month to attend meetings of the Georgia Department of Human Resources.

Mama rejected any security for the first couple of months, but then I decided that it would be necessary to include her as a member of my immediate family. The existing laws provide that the spouse and children of an incumbent president are protected — twenty-four hours every day. This idea was abhorrent to Mama, who declared that she would rather lock herself in her own house if threats really existed. The issue came to a head when I saw how valuable she was in attending state funerals for foreign leaders, and she made her first such trip, to India.

Fortunately, my successor as governor of Georgia was George Busbee, who had been my legislative floor leader and was a close friend. While Mama was in India, he offered to designate a member of the Georgia State Patrol as a security officer who would travel with Mama — if she would permit this intrusion on her privacy.

There was a state trooper who happened to be living in Plains named Ray Hathcock. He was also a farmer, and we had known him as a customer who bought fertilizer and seed from Carter's Warehouse. Without my knowing it, Ray had shown some interest in our family. In a recent interview, Ray provided some interesting insights into how he developed his relationship with Mama.

"As the time for the inauguration neared, I learned that the Americus High School band had been invited to march in the parade and that a local trooper was going to escort the band during the trip to Washington. I managed to convince the powers that be that this trip required two troopers, and I was permitted to go along. We became the only two state patrolmen who also marched in the inaugural parade, and we even attended the banquets and balls in the evening.

"When I was given the job of helping Miss Lillian, I picked her up at the airport after her trip to India. First thing she did was complain that her hands were very sore and for me not to let anyone touch them. The first few weeks were rough, because Miss Lillian really did not want anyone around her all the time."

Mama was bothered by the thousands of tourists who inundated Plains and who pressed in on her whenever she left her home. This created an unanticipated role for Ray.

He recalls, "What started out as a security job turned into a personal aide job as time went on and we got closer to each other. Pretty soon I was doing her shopping at the grocery store and, as she told everybody, the liquor store. I never let her run out of her favorite Old Forester bourbon. (She had one pretty strong toddy late every afternoon.) I would also go to her favorite clothing store, and the owners would pick out dresses and pantsuits that they thought she would like. I would carry them all back to her, and in a couple of days I would take the ones she did not want back to the store with a blank check for the ones she kept.

"One time I went to the bank and picked up some checks she had ordered. Nobody looked at the actual checks, and she immediately started paying bills. In a couple of weeks she began getting calls and letters from some people in Jacksonville, Florida, saying that she was writing checks on their account. After the new checks were printed, it took about a week to get everybody paid back."

Mother acquired a new friend when a wealthy Filipino, Amado Araneta, bought a large farm just on the edge of Plains. Among other things, he owned a sporting arena and a number of sugar mills in the Philippines, but he did not get along with President Ferdinand Marcos. His oldest son managed the family's business affairs back home while Amado chose to live in New York City. Gloria and Billy monitored Mother's relationship with Mr. Araneta as closely as possible and kept me informed. On one of my visits to Plains, I was amazed at how lively and effervescent my mother was when they were together.

Ray reports,

"Mr. Araneta bought Miss Lillian nice gifts and always insisted that she go out to dinner with his group when he visited the farm. If he stayed a week, that meant about five nights eating out. I was always glad to see him go home, as his visits cut into my personal social life. I had to do my dating on nights that Miss Lillian had no plans. Sometimes I did not know until late in the afternoon whether I was free that night. She would ask me what plans I had, and if she found out I had a date, she would not speak for a while. Miss Lillian enjoyed those nights out, and her eyes always lit up when she heard Mr. Araneta was in town. We visited the Aranetas one time in New York at their Fifth Avenue apartment."

For all the remaining time I was in Washington, Ray Hathcock stayed with my mother and played an increasing role in her affairs. During the campaign months of 1978, she made several speeches almost every day on behalf of Democratic candidates. Ray recalls, "After the first few speeches I heard her give, I sort of memorized them and remembered what she had said and where she had been. She had me start sitting in the front row in front of her, and if she forgot the name of something or someone, I would whisper it to her to refresh her memory."

When tourist pressures became unbearable for Mama in Plains, she decided to live almost full-time at the Pond House. Billy had the same problem and bought a home in a remote area about twenty miles from Plains, but from Gloria's home it would be only a ten-minute drive to reach Mama in an emergency. Also, there was a small security contingent at our home in Plains even when we were in Washington. Ray had a special telephone installed in Mama's bedroom that would ring them when the receiver was off the hook. This proved to be helpful in 1980, when Mama fell and broke her hip, knocking the phone off the table.

My mother had strong and almost unchangeable likes and dislikes, and she never made any attempt to conceal her feelings. Ray was present on one such occasion:

"Miss Lillian and I flew out of Albany on a trip, and when we walked into the air terminal, there stood Hugh Carter with a crowd of people. Hugh was the president's first cousin and a state senator, but at this time Miss Lillian was mad with Hugh about a book that he had written.* She accused Hugh of including private — and false — family information in his book. She walked right straight toward Hugh, and I got out of the way because I knew what was about to

* The book was titled *Cousin Beedie and Cousin Hot,* the nicknames that Hugh and I used in talking to one another.

180

happen. She tore into Hugh with no mercy, using some really harsh language. Hugh just stood there grinning while taking it. When she got through, I rejoined her and we boarded our flight. Hugh loved the encounter, as it made the local paper the next day, and more books were sold."

By this time Ray had become one of Mama's favorites, and he describes his first Christmas with her:

"To show how thoughtful Miss Lillian was, she sent me out to get a Christmas gift for her grandson Buddy Carter and told me to get him the nicest one I could find. I chose one of the new Polaroid flip cameras and had it gift-wrapped. It was just a family affair, and I didn't expect a present, but there was one for me. When I opened it, in a different wrapping, it was that camera. I had bought my own Christmas present. I can't remember what Buddy got."

Mama liked all kinds of music and was eager to meet the star performers when she became famous. She had met Bob Dylan when he visited the Governor's Mansion, and Elvis Presley after one of his performances in Atlanta. Ray reported that, in addition to those she knew in Las Vegas, Mama met country music stars who came to perform monthly in nearby Leslie, Georgia.

I was never involved in the arrangements with the state of Georgia that permitted Ray to be with Mama, but he has informed me about his impression of some questions that began to be raised.

"After two years, we had a change in leadership of the Georgia State Patrol, and the new director felt that it was not right for the state of Georgia to foot the expenses for a trooper doing this job. My salary continued, but they cut off my expense account, so the Carter family had to pick it up in order for me to stay. The president stopped me from staying in the expensive hotels in Washington and gave me a room at the White House. With this arrangement, I survived the politics of the Georgia State Patrol two more years."

Ray summarized his time with my mother this way: "We traveled in about a dozen foreign countries and in all the states except Alaska, North Dakota, and Hawaii, and traveling with Miss Lillian was great. You never knew what to expect. She never complained, regardless of how difficult it was sometimes, and one of the first things she told me when we started traveling was to never complain, regardless of how bad the food was or the service or the situation, just to smile and tell them how great it was. She did all of her complaining to me after we were back in our rooms. She was kind to everyone she met, but if she did not like something or someone, she would let you know it. She also was very jealous of other women getting the attention if she was around. She always managed to arrange to be the 'Star of the Show.' I was glad to be in the supporting cast."

14
AMERICA'S FIRST MAMA

In the White House, I kept a personal record of opinions and events that I knew would not be made public in the weekly reports of the official activities of a president. When I returned to Plains in 1981, I discovered that there were more than five thousand pages. I used this wealth of information as the basis for my presidential memoir, *Keeping Faith,* and for this book I have reviewed the entries concerning my mother. She was a frequent visitor to the White House, always demanding to stay in the Queen's Bedroom, immediately across the hall from the more famous Lincoln Bedroom. Mama had a good time on her own initiative, but I also called on her for a number of official state missions — which she later reminded me were mostly to represent our nation at funerals of distinguished foreign leaders.

A 1977 *New York Times* article about my mother reported, without explanation,

"During the last two centuries only thirty-eight women have achieved her pinnacle of maternal eminence, some posthumously if not accidentally. However, most of them really do appear to deserve a certain measure of credit for their sons' ascent, and in the case of the current title-holder the evidence is especially interesting and convincing."

I was surprised to learn after my election that Mama had played a key role in my crucial support from African Americans. One news article reported,

According to many pundits, Jimmy Carter never would have made it to the White House without the help of one particular black man: Andrew Young, former Representative from Georgia and current chief United States delegate to the United Nations. The story of how Mr. Young first came to trust a white Governor of Georgia has a definite bearing on the course of recent history.

As Mr. Young recalls it, he had met the Governor only once, briefly, before he himself decided in 1970 to run for Congress from a predominantly white district of Atlanta.

With no political experience except what he'd gained as a close aide of the late

Dr. Martin Luther King, Jr., Young was so startled to receive an unsolicited check at his campaign headquarters — mailed from the red clay of Sumter County by the Governor's mother — that he went to see her. And heard all about her experiences in the Peace Corps.

"She's the kind of woman you fall in love with," Andy Young explains.

So the next time he met her son, Mr. Young, who'd previously been sure that "nothing good could come from South Georgia, especially Plains," paid closer attention. This eventually led to his supporting Jimmy Carter and, among other consequences, to his own appointment to the United Nations.

When I had been in office less than a month, I was informed that Fakhruddin Ali Ahmed, President of India, had died. I decided that Mother would be perfect as the head of a large U.S. delegation to attend the funeral. When I called her at home in Plains, I first asked her what she was doing. She said she wasn't feeling well and was planning to go see a doctor. I said, "How would you like to go to India?" She said, "I'd love to go someday. Why?" And I said, "How about this afternoon?" She said,

"Okay, I'll be ready."

I told her that an air force plane would be at an airport in nearby Albany in four hours to pick her up, and that our son Chip, Senator Charles Percy, and about twenty other political leaders would join her at Andrews Air Force Base in Washington. She said she didn't have anything to wear, and I promised that one of the stores in Washington would have a selection of black dresses waiting at the airport. I did not have a chance to see her before she and the delegation left for India, but I was informed that she was pleased with one of the dresses.

The next day I talked to Mama on the phone while her plane was flying over Iran. At Rosalynn's suggestion, I told them that I could have the plane stop at Bombay after the funeral if Mother wanted to visit the site of her Peace Corps work. She was delighted, and I made the arrangements.

While in New Delhi, Mother had a long meeting with Prime Minister Indira Gandhi, whom she had always disliked because of her adherence to the caste system and, at least indirectly, because she had delayed my mother, as a Peace Corps volunteer working on family planning, from serving in the medical clinic. Mama reported, "Mrs. Gandhi was so charming to me." Asked by news reporters what she thought about Gandhi's party having lost the recent election, she responded, "No comment. Jimmy asked me the same question, and I gave him the same answer. He said, 'But I'm your son, the President of the United States, and you know about India.' I repeated, 'No comment.'"

The highlight of the trip, for Mama and her companions, was the visit to her Peace Corps village, Vikhroli. Mama arrived with great excitement and appreciation. "I can't wait to kiss everybody," she said. She was embarrassed and crestfallen when no one was there to meet her. She recovered quickly however, and said to the American delegation, "Well, we can just walk down the street and around the corner, and I'll show y'all the apartment where I used to stay."

When they made the turn, there were more than ten thousand people waiting in complete silence; they then burst into an uproarious welcome. Old friends greeted her as "Lilly behn" (our sister Lilly), and there was a carefully rehearsed program of songs, dancing, and yoga exercises. After the required public exchanges of greetings and a gift of lovely Indian sandals, Mama commented to the crowd, "I never knew you thought so much of me. I'm so excited that I had forgotten that Jimmy is president. I didn't even care. The first time I came here, I walked so much it seemed like a thousand miles, but I give you my word, I was happier walking here, sometimes barefoot, than I am now coming in the president's plane."

She then requested a visit to the clinic where she had served. One man, a former patient, came forward to tell her that his asthma was much better. "Of course," teased Mama, "I cured you." As she visited one patient after another, she was heard to murmur, "I feel like an angel, but I know I'm not."

When Mother returned home, I gave her an assessment from the State Department that the trip was a superb diplomatic effort and that we had the best relations now with India that we'd had since 1960, largely because of her visit and her obvious concern for the Indian people.

Three weeks later, Mother received a bill for $450 for the black dress. She exploded and called the White House demanding to speak to me immediately. I was in an important cabinet meeting, and the operator asked if Mama could call back later. She refused, telling the operator that it was a family emergency. I was called to the telephone, fearing some personal catastrophe in Plains. Mama yelled that she was not going to pay for any damn dress that she wore on a state

Our family enjoyed Christmas together, 1977

mission. In order to resume my duties, I told her to send the bill to me, and I paid for the dress.

My next diary entry concerning my mother was in April: "I decided to take my mother out for the evening. It's the first time I remember since I've been married . . . more than thirty years . . . that I've taken Mama out, just the two of us. We went to see Howard Keel in *Shenandoah* and we enjoyed being with each other."

Mother spent the next few months working with Gloria on the collection of several hundred letters she had sent home while in the Peace Corps. I read a proof copy of the book, and it brought back all the memories we'd had while she was gone. The letters provided a remarkable insight into Mother's experiences while she was there. Mama celebrated her seventy-ninth birthday while she and Gloria were on an extensive tour to promote their book.

Mother received many awards, honorary doctorates, and other honors during her lifetime, but she seemed proudest of a ceremony in New York in September 1977, when she was recognized as the Outstanding Humanitarian of the Year with an eighteen-thousand-dollar stipend (which she gave to charity). It was by the United Jewish Appeal, and after an elaborate "This Is Your Life" presentation, she stood and said, "I've never been with so many Jews before in my life, and I love you all." She got a standing ovation.

No matter where she was, Mother always kept abreast of sporting events, especially baseball, tennis, wrestling, and college football in the Southeast. She was extremely happy when her beloved L.A. Dodgers were National League champions and faced the New York Yankees in the World Series. She immediately modified her book tour schedule so that she could be in Los Angeles for two games.

Richard Harden, Shirley MacLaine, Mama,
and her security guard, Ray Hathcock, 1978

One of her proudest moments was when she threw out the first ball at the fourth game of the series in Dodger Stadium. She had stayed up until the early morning hours the previous night, talking to Shirley Mac-Laine, a special friend. During the game, George Steinbrenner invited her to sit in his box when the teams returned to New York for the final contests, and Mama canceled other events to make this possible. On the way to the East Coast, she stopped in Las Vegas to appear on the Johnny Carson show. Johnny commented that I had dropped in the public opinion polls. Mama replied,

A Down-Home Barnes Dance

Join
Miz Lillian Carter

Three Days to Victory!

Mike Barnes for Congress

Barnes for Congress
8525 Colesville Road
Silver Spring, Maryland 20910

Edward Sanders
Special Asst. to the President
The White House
D.C. 20500

Sweetwater
String Band

Footloose Cloggers

JOIN
MIZ LILLIAN CARTER
IN SUPPORTING
MIKE BARNES FOR CONGRESS
THREE DAYS TO VICTORY!

POLITICAL AUCTION
A chance to own reminders of our Democratic
campaign heritage and to participate in our
political present.

REFRESHMENTS

**Saturday, November 4
4 to 6 p.m.**
For reservations!
Mail the attached coupon
or call 589-6111

Longwood Community Center
19300 Ga. Ave.
Olney, Md.
1.8 mile past Olney on left

Miz Lillian and the Barnes Dance
Enclosed is $ _____ for _____ admissions at $10 each.
Enclosed is $ _____ for _____ Senior Citizen admissions at $5 each.

Name _____

Address _____

Occupation _____

Principal place of business _____

**I cannot attend, but enclosed
is my contribution of $ _____ .**

Make checks payable to:
Barnes for Congress Committee
8525 Colesville Road
Silver Spring, Maryland 20910
589-6111

*Mama campaigned throughout the nation in 1978 for
Democratic candidates for governor and Congess.*

"Johnny, I noticed lately that your ratings have dropped worse than Jimmy's." For her, the Dodgers' final loss was almost assuaged by seeing Reggie Jackson hit three home runs in the game, tying a fifty-year record set by Babe Ruth.

Mother took several trips to Europe on her own, sometimes just informing us when all the plans were made or after she returned. She was quite interested in the Friendship Force, which promoted visiting in private homes in foreign nations for about a week and then receiving host families for return visits in the States. Mama made several visits to Newcastle upon Tyne, in England, and one of her trips was to "that place that makes snuff." I eventually realized that she was talking about Copenhagen, Denmark. Her favorite destination was Ireland, and she formed a permanent love affair with the country and its people. She called me from Belfast and then Dublin, saying that she didn't want to come back home, and that if she could have another month there she could resolve the problem between the Catholics and the Protestants.

In July 1978 my mother was awarded the Ceres Medal by the Food and Agriculture Organization of the United Nations for her extensive humanitarian service. Other women recipients of the medal included Prime Minister Indira Gandhi, Mother Teresa, and two queens.

This became an event that Mama stretched out as a maximum experience. When they first informed her that she had won the award, the sponsors offered to come to America to make the presentation. But Mama immediately declared, "I'm going to Rome." During her briefings, she was informed that invitations had come for her to visit some of the countries in West Africa that had been devastated by extreme drought. She was delighted to accept, and Gambia, Senegal, Mali, and Upper Volta were added to her itinerary. She then suggested that, since they were Francophone nations, a further briefing in Paris would be helpful, and stops there and then in Morocco were added.

In Paris she met with French President Giscard d'Estaing, foreign ministry leaders, and U.S. Ambassador Arthur Hartman, and found time to go shopping and to experience some of the nightlife. She and some embassy personnel attended a risqué floor show, part of which consisted of scantily dressed men and women cavorting on roller skates. Mama and the ambassador were at a choice table adjoining the stage, and one of the male performers "slipped" and wound up in Mama's lap, with his arms around her neck. Perhaps not coincidentally, a photographer snapped their picture. The ambassador had to use his diplomatic wiles to obtain the film before it was distributed to the news media.

During and after my political campaigns, Mama had developed a reputation for expressing unorthodox opinions and not being constrained by any outside advice. When she traveled overseas on behalf of our government, the officials in the State Department were always quite nervous about what she would do or say that might violate protocol and damage relations between our government and that of the country she was visiting. None of her family members were surprised when suggested speech notes were completely ignored.

Italy was an especially troublesome case, with its rapidly changing governments, apparent successes of the Communist Party, and a sensitive U.S. diplomatic relationship with the Vatican. As their plane approached the airport in Rome, her traveling companions attempted to give Mama some written suggestions, but she brushed them all aside. "I've already thought of something to say," she said.

Surrounded by the news media, Mama

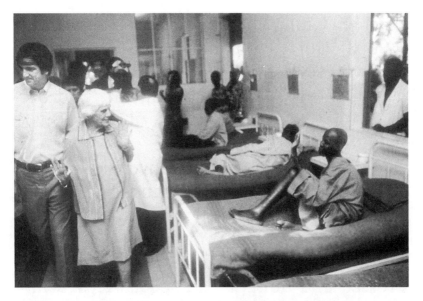

Richard Harden and Mama visit a hospital in West Africa, 1978

declared, "I am here to receive the cherished Ceres award, and am delighted to be in Italy, for three reasons: First, I understand you have just chosen a fine young president whom I have been eager to meet since my husband passed away. [President Alessandro Pertini was two years older than my mother.] Second, as a former Methodist and now a Baptist, my highest religious ambition will be realized when I have my scheduled conversation with the Pope. And third, I have never met an ugly Italian."

I received a message from U.S. Ambassador Richard Gardner in Italy describing the superlative job that Mother did in meeting with the new president. I never found out what they talked about.

Pope Paul VI was not in the Vatican, but he invited Mother to visit at his summer palace. For this special occasion, she had borrowed a black dress, as described by Billy's wife, Sybil:

"Miss Lillian chose a relatively long dress, with thin shoulder straps and a somewhat fancy jacket. We both thought that it was both attractive and appropriate for a papal visit. At her hotel in Rome, she had the dress pressed and hung it in a special closet, illuminated so that clothing could be carefully selected. When Miss Lillian went to get the dress, smoke was coming out of the closet. She found that the jacket had slipped from the hanger and was lying on a hot lightbulb that had been installed in the floor. There was a big hole burned in the shoulder. It was too late to go shopping, so she put on the damaged outfit and carefully arranged a large shawl around her neck so that it covered the burned hole. She practiced how to pull the shawl to cover her head for the interview without revealing the damaged jacket, and survived the visit quite well. Later, in lieu of buying me a good dress, she gave me the shawl, on which the Pope had placed his hand during his blessing."

Mama enjoyed the visit with the Pope.

Mama enjoyed crowds of well-wishers in West Africa.

She had practiced on what to call him. She recalled later, "I concentrated on 'Holy Father,' not 'Your Majesty' or 'Your Excellency,' but after a few minutes I don't even remember what title I used. I'm not a Catholic, you know, and never knew but one down in Plains, but I decided on the spot that I never felt so close to God as looking at that man's face." They talked about age. She was eighty, and he was eighty-one. He told her, "I am now ready to meet God." This was one of the last private meetings the Pope had before his death.

When Pope Paul asked if she had any special requests, Mother reported that she had stopped in Paris to learn all she could about the Sub-Saharan region, which was suffering from a severe drought. She and His Holiness shared a prayer for some climatic relief. Later, she told a reporter, "If I had my life to live over again, I'd be a Catholic. I'm a Baptist, and they don't believe in having a drink late in the afternoon, or playing poker — things I love to do."

Her next stop was Rabat, Morocco, where Mother was invited to dine with King Hassan II. She said that they had a delightful talk, and he offered her a collection of perfumes. She thanked him but declined, saying that she had too much luggage already. The king responded that he had a state visit scheduled in Washington and would deliver it himself.

Mother never forgot any of the details of her visits to the West African nations, where she had her first real experience with black people in their native lands. Presidents Jawara (Gambia), Senghor (Senegal), Lamizana (Upper Volta), and Traoré (Mali) were

Our family posed for a White House photograph, 1979

very gracious to her, and were especially impressed with her knowledge of both medicine and agriculture. She knew all about cotton, groundnuts, and maize, and even pretended to enjoy a long trip to spend an hour or two at a chicken farm. She told the people there that Daddy used to buy two hundred baby chicks at a time that ran loose in our yard. She requested a visit to Timbuktu while in Mali, and it was on this trip that the entire region was blessed by a tremendous rain — up to five inches in some places. Now, more than twenty-five years later, some of the leaders remind me that Pope Paul and my mother brought their people relief from that memorable drought.

After she returned home from Africa, the National Democratic Committee asked Mother to go on the campaign trail for congressional candidates, and she spent three or four days a week visiting some of the most important and closely contested districts.

She interrupted her political assignments to attend the world heavyweight championship fight between Muhammad Ali and Leon Spinks, as a guest of John Amos, the founder of Aflac insurance company. She was delighted when her friend Ali regained his world title with a fifteen-round unanimous decision.

When Israel's former prime minister Golda Meir died, I asked Mother to represent me as head of the delegation to the funeral. She said she had already promised to be in Los Angeles to help with some political campaigns but would go to Israel if I could get her out of this commitment. At Ben-Gurion Airport, Mama was told that Mrs. Meir had requested no eulogies. *The New York Times* reported that Mama raised her eyes and said, "Golda, this is not a eulogy to you. This is just me telling you how I wish I had known you."

Mama returned to Washington in time for the state visit of Morocco's King Hassan, who stayed in the White House with two of his sons. She was in the Queen's Bedroom and the king was in the Lincoln Bedroom, and during the state banquet he reminded her of his promised gift of perfume when she had visited his country. They bantered back and forth, almost as old friends, and afterward she was invited to the king's room, where he presented her with a nice bottle. He then said, "There are twenty-one other scents in this case, and you can take your pick, including the entire collection." Mama responded, "No, thanks. That would be too much." And then she laughed. "You damn foreigners are all just alike!" He laughed also, put his arms around her, and gave her a kiss on her cheek. I doubt that the king had ever been called a "damn foreigner" before, and I don't know anyone else who could have gotten away with it.

15

PLAINS VS.
THE WHITE HOUSE

Rosalynn and I were able to get back home to Plains several times a year while I was president, and I spent as much time as possible with my mother. Instead of our sitting around a coffee table for long discussions, she usually insisted on having conversations in a boat, while fishing. She would choose the place to fish, and she invariably caught more bass and bream than I did. She relished commenting on my fishing technique, usually claiming, "Jimmy, you just pull too quick." My excuse was that she was regularly learning the best fishing holes while I had to be in Washington running the nation's affairs.

Near the end of a prolonged stay in the White House while she recovered from a bout with phlebitis, Mother commented that she did not feel imprisoned there but did feel like a prisoner when she was back in Plains. "The place is now overrun with tourists, and

I don't have a moment of peace. With you and Rosalynn in Washington, they all want to get to *me,* and they even line up to peek in my front window when I'm trying to watch my soap operas. However, I'm going home to Plains this weekend because my dog is in obedience school and his time is up. He's already smarter than I am." Back home, she began moving more of her personal things out to the Pond House, where she was to live the rest of her life, leaving downtown Plains.

After declining several invitations, Mama finally agreed to meet with the Washington press corps in January 1979. The top news in the city at that time was about Billy having escorted some Libyan officials on a visit to Plains. It was an unorthodox occasion for my mother, who wore a blue floor-length shirtwaist dress and turned down a bourbon and water when she first arrived.

She showed the assembled reporters a few slides from her visit to the Sahel area of West Africa and then prepared for questions. "I just left Jimmy, and he said, 'Mother, be prepared,' and I said, 'Prepared for what?' I know you wouldn't ask me anything nasty." They began with a polite question, "Miss Lillian, where are you going next?" She replied that it seemed that most of her assignments were to attend state funerals, and she couldn't predict who would be the next to die. Then came a question about Billy and how she explained his behavior.

"That's a difficult question for a mother to answer," she said slowly. "I've tried to raise my children right and proper, to do what's best, to live with God's help. I can't control what they do when they are grown. Billy loves everybody and I believe him when he says that. If he has offended anybody, I hope it doesn't hurt."

To change the subject, the next question was, "How much time do you spend in Washington?"

"No more than I have to."

"Weren't you once quoted as saying Billy was your favorite child?"

"Oh, I've said that about all of them at one time or another. I don't always agree with what they say, but I don't have to."

Mother also reported that she and I had a five-dollar bet on the Super Bowl game that Sunday. She was for the Pittsburgh Steelers, and she offered her opinion on the cheerleaders' costumes. "If my daughter was out there, I would hope she would freeze to death."

Discussing her multiple visits to the White

*Anwar Sadat, Menachem Begin, and their wives
joined our family, 1979*

House, Mama confessed that she had enjoyed meeting charming men. She described President Anwar Sadat of Egypt as "my favorite of all the men in the world," and added that she also found Johnny Carson particularly appealing. "I like Johnny Carson. I thought he was an ass until I met him. He's a very intelligent, a very sensitive man."

Mama also had a very good relationship with Menachem Begin. He and I had this recorded telephone exchange after he visited with Sadat in April 1979. We exchanged our normal greetings:

Menachem Begin: My wife and I send our best wishes equally to Rosalynn, Amy, and to your mother.

JC: My mother will never forget your embracing her first after the peace treaty signing ceremony.

MB: All the time she was sending kisses to me in the air! The evening in the tent was beautiful.

Mother was invited to receive a number of honorary doctorates, and I advised her to accept a few of them. She always preferred to make speeches to university audiences in more informal settings. This alternative was also easier on the rest of the family, because she expected some of us to be present when she received special honors. When possible, I would just write a letter of congratulations to be read on these occasions.

In August 1979, it was becoming increasingly evident that Senator Ted Kennedy would be challenging me for the Democratic presidential nomination, and Mama was quite concerned. Soon thereafter, she had pains in her left shoulder and chest, and we convinced her to enter the hospital for a

The visit of Pope John Paul II to the White House, 1979

thorough physical examination. I flew home to Plains to visit her, and the doctors said that she was suffering from intense discomfort but they believed her ailment was either bursitis or arthritis. She was soon feeling better, and I returned to Washington, sure that she would join us in plenty of time for the upcoming visit by the new Pope, John Paul II.

Mother ranked this meeting as one of her most memorable occasions. Recounting their introduction at a White House reception, she said, "I had on high heels and the floor had just been waxed. I walked in the room and skidded right across the floor. Jimmy laughed and kissed me, and poor Rosalynn turned red as fire. I said to the Pope, 'Holy Father, I made this dramatic entrance just for you.' He laughed and said, 'I enjoyed it very much.'"

After an enormous reception for His Holiness on the South Lawn, he returned to our private quarters for a meeting with my immediate family. He commented on Mother having been one of the last visitors received by his predecessor and gave her a parchment copy of his first encyclical letter. He seemed to consider it more significant than my silver sculpture saying PEACE UNTO THEE and papal medals received by all the others.

Mama went home for a few days and then returned to the White House for the visit of Jack Lynch, Prime Minister of Ireland, and his wife, Máirín. Rosalynn couldn't be there, and the State Department suggested that Mother serve as the official hostess because she had visited Ireland several times and knew the government officials. We had a big crowd at the welcoming ceremony, and the prime minister reminded us that 12 percent of our nation's citizens are Irish Americans — not including those who are Scots Irish. He seemed to consider my mother as

*Mother joined me in hosting the official visit
of Ireland's Prime Minister Lynch, 1979*

Ireland's special ambassador in the White House.

In November 1979 a group of American diplomats had been taken captive by young militants in Iran. I was blamed for our inability to return them to freedom, and public opinion polls reported that Senator Ted Kennedy was leading me by a three-to-one margin. Mother and Rosalynn began campaigning again, starting in New Hampshire and working their way westward. Early in December I was surprised to receive a phone call from Muhammad Ali, who was in Las Vegas with Mama. She had told him that I might need a prominent Muslim to reach the Ayatollah Khomeini, and Ali wanted to offer his services to seek the hostages' freedom. Later, I had some of our national security officials talk to him, and he made a strong effort, but his and all others were rejected.

Mama, continuing her campaigning, just happened to be in Pasadena, California, in time to support her team, the Pittsburgh Steelers, in the Super Bowl. Not surprisingly, at least to our family, the score was Steelers 31, Los Angeles Rams 19.

Her next scheduled state for campaigning was Maine, and Mama called me in advance, uncharacteristically nervous because she had heard this was strong Kennedy territory. I assured her that she would find a good reception up there and advised her just to enjoy herself and not say anything negative about the senator.

After three very successful days in New England, Mama was scheduled to go to Nashville, Tennessee, where she joined Tom T. Hall, Johnny Cash, and other country music stars for political rallies and a fundraiser. In fact, she had a great time in both parts of the country. She did well, except that she told a news reporter that, if she had a million dollars, she would take out a contract on Ayatollah Khomeini. I guess that this was her version of a fatwa.

Nevertheless, I could tell Mama was somewhat tired of the campaign trail when she called to remind me that I was beating Kennedy by a margin of two to one and to tell me that she had an invitation from Labor Secretary Ray Marshall to accompany him to a global women's employment seminar in Paris. She had decided to go from there to Israel for a few days of visiting holy places, en route to accept a personal invitation from President Sadat to tour some ancient sites in Egypt. She called every day or two during her trip to receive further good news about the Democratic primary returns, and discouraging information about the plight of our hostages in Iran.

Mother had met Marshal Josip Broz Tito of Yugoslavia when he paid an official visit to our country in 1978, and it was natural that she join Vice President Walter Mondale as a leader of our distinguished delegation to his funeral, soon after she returned from her tour of Israel and Egypt. This was probably the most massive international event in which Mama played a role, as she joined representatives from more than 125 nations in paying honor to the deceased leader. Tito had been able to stand up against fascism, to hold six disparate ethnic groups together, to defy pressure from his fellow Communists in the Soviet Union, and to serve as one of the founders of the developing nations' Group of Seventy-seven. Mother especially enjoyed her conversations with Ambassador Averell Harriman during the trip to Belgrade, which she said was much more interesting than having listened to Tito's forty-minute toast (which then had to be translated) at the White House banquet.

As the time for the 1980 Democratic National Convention approached, it was obvious that I had easily overcome the challenge from Senator Kennedy, but our family members were afflicted by personal allegations that were quite distressing to my mother. There were some widely publicized criticisms of my sister Ruth Carter Stapleton because she had visited Oman and one or two other Islamic countries during one of her evangelical tours. This is something she had done extensively on all continents long before I became involved in national politics.

The politically inspired allegations were that Ruth was too cozy with Arab leaders who were not friendly to Israel. The motivation of the accusers was obviously to hurt me politically, and I wasn't concerned, but Mother seemed to be upset. We decided that it would be good to have both Mother and Ruth interviewed by Walter Cronkite, since they had been jointly involved in Ruth's evangelical ministry. Almost overnight following their answers to Cronkite's questions, the issue disappeared from the news.

Billy didn't fare so well in addressing the accusation that he was involved as something of a lobbyist for the regime of Muammar al-Qaddafi in Libya. Ultimately, full Senate hearings were held on the subject, in an effort by some members to involve me. Although Billy had attempted to obtain a contract for some Libyan oil to be sold in America, he made it clear that he had never informed me about his activities. He maintained that my holding office as governor and president had been detrimental to his business and personal life. The media furor was not assuaged, even when I held a full White House press conference and answered questions exclusively on this subject for more than an hour.

In addition to all this, there were completely false and unfounded accusations that I had been involved in an improper sexual relationship with one of our friends at home. All of these allegations were repugnant to my mother and severely dampened her enthusiasm for politics, but she joined our other

215

supporters after Labor Day in campaigning around the country.

I had a long and enjoyable conversation with Mother on October 1, my birthday, and she gave me an interesting and humorous report on some of her experiences. From the reactions of people she was meeting, she was convinced that I would win reelection easily. The next day, however, she fell and fractured her right hip, and the doctors told me that it was a very serious injury that would require surgery and a long recuperation. Her most persistent question was "How soon can I be fishing again at the Pond House?" and her greatest concern was whether the Dodgers would be playing in the World Series.

Recalling how she had first learned that I was projected to lose the 1980 election, Mama said, "I was in the hospital with a broken hip when Jimmy came to my room and said he was going to lose. It was the day before the election, and all the news was about the anniversary of the hostages being held in Iran, and blaming it on Jimmy. I said, 'Good!' and I went to sleep. I wanted him out — my whole family had been attacked and split wide open from Jimmy being president."

I had never really known that my mother felt this way and at first blamed it on the hostage crisis and her broken hip, but then I recalled an interview in late 1979, when she was told that Senator Kennedy might run against me for the Democratic nomination. She commented, "If he does run, I wish him all the luck in the world and hope to goodness nothing happens to him." When questioned about this a few days later, she explained, "I only had Teddy's health in mind."

16
BACK AT HOME

Although she was a registered nurse who had operated a nursing home herself, Mother was a surprisingly difficult hospital patient. It was not possible for her to relax, concentrate on her physical therapy, and accept the necessary restraints on her activities. Billy, Gloria, Sybil, and her granddaughter Kim visited her every day, and I called often, but we were not able to satisfy her insatiable demand for news and attention.

I flew to Wiesbaden, Germany, the day after leaving the White House to greet the American hostages, who had been freed by the Iranians just five minutes after I was no longer president. They had been sitting at the end of a runway in Tehran since early that morning, after I had spent three days and two nights negotiating their release. I embraced them all, and one of them said he had escorted my mother during her visit to Morocco and wanted to send her a message.

All I had in my pocket was the notes I had used for welcoming the hostages to freedom, and he wrote on the back his greetings to her. Mama was delighted when she received the note.

Back in Plains, it seemed obvious to me that Mother's full recovery would be expedited if she moved from the hospital to the nursing home in Plains — the former Wise Sanitarium, where she had received her training and then practiced as a nurse. She finally agreed to this unanimous recommendation from our family members and began to make much more rapid progress in walking again.

She also agreed to let a few news reporters visit her for interviews. One of the most extensive was with *McCall's* magazine, in which she said she was not at all disappointed that I was defeated for reelection. Claiming she was often bored at the White House, she said that she could finally tell the truth, because when she'd said this earlier, "Jimmy started sending me all over the place, mostly to funerals, running my legs off." Like all the rest of us, Mama may have been trying to rationalize the election results — or maybe she was just trying to be controversial.

By the first of March, Mama could take a few steps even without the walker, and she

Mother and her chidren: Billy, Ruth, Gloria, and Jimmy, 1981

insisted on returning to the Pond House. (We had converted her house in Plains into an office for my use.) The doctors finally let her return to the isolated cabin, with the understanding that she have a full-time practical nurse, continue her therapy, and fish only from a chair on the pier and not in a boat.

My diary entry for April 17, 1981, reads: "I picked up Mama at the nursing home and took her to the Pond House. She was very excited about being home. I think this will really help her if she doesn't get too adventurous. I've never seen her any happier than she is to be back at the pond."

When Mama demonstrated her ability to walk from her chair to the bed and back without any mechanism to help her, I told her we would pave her driveway down to the mailbox and also a path around the edge of the pond so she could go fishing without assistance. By the time this project was finished, she was able to take full advantage of it.

I spent most of my first year at home getting our financial affairs in order, renewing my involvement in our farming operation, writing my presidential memoir, raising private funds to build a presidential library, and initiating the work of The Carter Center. I had been an avid runner since my days on the Naval Academy cross-country team and was jogging five or six miles each day back in Plains. Most of my early morning runs were by the Pond House, and I enjoyed stopping in for an almost daily conversation with my mother.

During that summer, Mama was able to join Rosalynn and me in hosting Egyptian President Anwar Sadat and later Israeli Prime Minister Menachem Begin on their visits to Plains. She enjoyed being the center of attention as both of the leaders spent much of their time discussing their previous visits with her.

Mother preferred to do her own cooking and the normal work around the house, but she agreed to permit a maid to come each day, provided she would stay only three hours. The maid's primary duties were picking up the mail, buying groceries, and making visits to the library. Still relatively immobile compared with her previous years, Mama managed to lead a full life. She followed all kinds of sporting events and world news on her satellite television, maintained a constant stream of correspondence, built up large monthly telephone bills, and still had plenty of time for fishing.

Mother once told reporters that going to church was the only social affair available in Plains, and that all our lives were centered on religion. She was reported as saying: "When Jimmy was sixteen, they asked him to teach Sunday School in our church and he was thrilled. He never thought he'd get that high in the world."

In fact, social life in Plains was as full as in Atlanta or Washington. For women, there were two garden clubs, a literary club, the Junior Women's Club, the Red Hat Club, a group of widows who call themselves PALS, and the most exclusive, Stitch and Chat. Mama avoided most of them, saying, "I'm not a joiner. I go to church on Sunday. We have a little club, the Stitch 'n' Chat. But that's the only thing I go to. I like for the ladies to go to the garden clubs, but I'm not interested — in gardening." One of Mama's friends, Lilloise Sheffield, said, "There's more to do here in Plains than there is time to do it in."

Mama had always been an accomplished bridge player, but she preferred her regular Thursday afternoon poker games. All the ladies used dimes instead of poker chips and had identical canvas bank bags in which they kept their stakes from one week to the next. They were expert players and very serious about the outcome of the games. We soon learned to watch the size of Mama's bag and to stay away from her, at least for a few hours, when she came home with her bag less than half full.

The next big struggle, which lasted for more than a year, was convincing Mama that she could not drive her car again. She finally agreed, provided that she could keep the car and that one of her children or grandchildren would be available as her chauffeur when needed.

Because of her forceful and demanding personality, Mama remained the matriarch, as intimately involved as possible in the affairs of all her family.

In the summer of 1983, we learned that Ruth had contracted pancreatic cancer, the same disease that had caused our father's death. She attempted chemotherapy and more holistic treatments, including a special diet prescribed by a doctor in the Caribbean. Mother was able to go with us on our visits, but we had to acknowledge Ruth's obvious lack of progress.

When I arrived at the Pond House one morning that same summer, I found Mother quite distressed. She regularly examined her breasts and had just found a small lump. Within a few days, we learned that it was malignant and had seriously metastasized, even to her pancreas. Mother remained at the Pond House as long as possible but eventually became too ill to avoid constant hospital care. Surprisingly, she seemed more vibrant and happy after she accepted the prognosis — more interested in assuaging our concerns than bemoaning her impending death.

It was at this time, late in September, that we learned Ruth had died, and we had to attend the funeral services in North Carolina without our mother. When we returned home, it was obvious that Mama also was

Sybil and Mama on our visit with Ruth during her battle with pancreatic cancer. Both Mama and Ruth died soon afterward, in 1983.

prepared to die, but she stayed busy during her last days giving instructions to all of us about her private affairs — and also ours.

All of us assembled around the bedside during her final hours, during which she was both cheerful and alert. She dozed off every now and then, and passed away peacefully on October 30, at the age of eighty-five and just a month after Ruth's death. We followed her instructions for a very brief graveside burial service, attended by several hundred of her relatives and friends.

She had fifteen grandchildren and eight great-grandchildren.

Postscript, in Vikhroli

In October 2006, Rosalynn and I led several thousand volunteers on our twenty-fourth annual week of building homes for Habitat for Humanity. It has been our custom to alternate each year between America and a foreign nation, and this time we chose a site near Mumbai and Vikhroli, the village where Mother had served in the Peace Corps. Elaborate plans were made for our visit, with a tour of the factories and places where Mama had worked and lived, a beautiful meal, and an assembly of as many of her former associates as possible to greet us. We had never been there, and knew these people only through Mama's letters and her later verbal accounts. Some of the key ones assembled in a large circle and recounted to us their memories — from almost forty years earlier!

A younger generation of Godrej family members were still the owners, and they had on display a vast array of their manufactured products, from soap and furniture to satellite components. Dr. Bhatia and his wife described their medical practices, still treating large numbers of patients. We noticed many copies of the book *Away from Home: Letters to My Family* on the tables, with a cover photograph of Mama and the little daughter of Mr. Vinod. We asked about the former gardener who had been so generous in sharing vegetables and flowers. A beautiful and slender woman stood up and informed us that her father had died but that she was the little girl whom Mama had taught to read and write. She had received her doctorate and was now the president of a nearby university.

Our hearts filled with pride and our eyes with tears, as we thought about how many other lives had been affected by my mother.

ACKNOWLEDGMENTS

It has been a special pleasure to write about my mother because so many people who knew her have been eager to contribute their memories to this book. In addition to the members of our own family, I have enjoyed conversations with Richard Harden, Ray Hathcock, Dot Godwin, and a large number of others who knew Mama during the times when I was away from home in the navy or serving as governor and president. The staff at my presidential library in Atlanta has been especially helpful in sharing with me their archive of photographs, personal letters, diary notes, and official documents that described my mother's activities more fully.

Alice Mayhew and her staff at Simon & Schuster have worked closely with my assistant, Lauren Gay, in the editing of this final text.

ABOUT THE AUTHOR

Jimmy Carter was born in Plains, Georgia, and served as thirty-ninth President of the United States. He and his wife, Rosalynn, founded The Carter Center, a nonprofit organization that prevents and resolves conflicts, enhances freedom and democracy, and improves health around the world. He is the author of numerous books, including *An Hour Before Daylight,* called "an American classic," and the #1 *New York Times* bestseller *Our Endangered Values.*

The employees of Thorndike Press hope you have enjoyed this Large Print book. All our Thorndike and Wheeler Large Print titles are designed for easy reading, and all our books are made to last. Other Thorndike Press Large Print books are available at your library, through selected bookstores, or directly from us.

For information about titles, please call:

(800) 223-1244

or visit our Web site at:

http://gale.cengage.com/thorndike

To share your comments, please write:

Publisher
Thorndike Press
295 Kennedy Memorial Drive
Waterville, ME 04901